THE
FALL
OF
AMERICA

poems of these states
1965-1971

★

ALLEN GINSBERG

'. . . *same electric lightning South*
     follows this train
        Apocalypse prophesied —
   the fall of America
     signalled from Heaven —'

City Lights

the pocket poets series no. 30

ISBN: 978-0-87286-063-6

Library of Congress Catalog Card Number: 72-84228

CITY LIGHTS BOOKS are edited by Lawrence Ferlinghetti and Nancy J. Peters and published at the City Lights Bookstore, 261 Columbus Avenue, San Francisco, CA 94133.

Dedicated
to

WALT WHITMAN

"Intense and loving comradeship, the personal and passionate attachment of man to man—which, hard to define, underlies the lessons and ideals of the profound saviors of every land and age, and which seems to promise, when thoroughly develop'd, cultivated and recognised in manners and literature, the most substantial hope and safety of the future of these States, will then be fully express'd.

"It is to the development, identification, and general prevalence of that fervid comradeship, (the adhesive love, at least rivaling the amative love hitherto possessing imaginative literature, if not going beyond it,) that I look for the counterbalance and offset of our materialistic and vulgar American democracy, and for the spiritualization thereof. Many will say it is a dream, and will not follow my inferences: but I confidently expect a time when there will be seen, running like a half-hid warp through all the myriad audible and visible worldly interests of America, threads of manly friendship, fond and loving, pure and sweet, strong and life-long, carried to degrees hitherto unknown—not only giving tone to individual character, and making it unprecedentedly emotional, muscular, heroic, and refined, but having the deepest relations to general politics. I say democracy infers such loving comradeship, as its most inevitable twin or counterpart, without which it will be incomplete, in vain, and incapable of perpetuating itself."

Democratic Vistas, 1871

ACKNOWLEDGING that among other places these poems were printed first in *Evergreen Review, Pacific Nation, San Francisco Free Press, Fuori!, New American Review, Transatlantic, Partisan Review, Paris Review, New York Free Press, Liberation News Service, W.I.N. Magazine, Concerning Poetry, New York Quarterly, Caterpillar, Notes from Underground, The Stone, Berkeley Barb, Berkeley Tribe, Boulder Express, Scenes Along the Road, Sun Books Australia, The Seventies, Look, Capella Dublin, Buffalo Stamps, New York Times, Sing Out, Litteraturnya Gazette, Ashok Shahane, The World, Alternative Press, Alternative Features Syndicate, Holy Soul Jellyroll, East Village Other, Antioch Review, Rain, Coyote's Journal, Big Sky, Poetry Review London, Mikrokosmos, The Paris Magazine, Schism, Rolling Stone, The Marijuana Review, Fits, The American Poetry Review, The Unspeakable Visions of the Individual*, poet & publisher thank editor friends for conserving early texts.

Bibliographical Note

"Wichita Vortex Sutra" (in *Planet News,* City Lights Books, 1968) fits in sequence following "Hiway Poesy LA-Albuquerque-Texas-Wichita" in this book.

Iron Horse (Coach House Press, Toronto, 1973) fits in sequence at the beginning of the section "Zigzag Back Thru These States 1966-1967."

CONTENTS

Page

After Words

I

Thru the Vortex West Coast to East

1965-1966

BEGINNING OF A POEM OF THESE STATES

Memento for Gary Snyder

Under the bluffs of Oroville, blue cloud September
skies, entering U.S. border, red red apples bend their tree
boughs propt with sticks —
At Omak a fat girl in dungarees leads her big brown
horse by asphalt highway.
Thru lodgepole pine hills Coleville near Moses'
Mountain—a white horse standing back of a 2 ton truck
moving forward between trees.
At Nespelem, in the yellow sun, a marker for Chief
Joseph's grave under rilled brown hills—white cross over
highway.
At Grand Coulee under leaden sky, giant red genera-
tors humm thru granite & concrete to materialize onions —
And grey water laps against the grey sides of Steam-
boat Mesa.
At Dry Falls 40 Niagaras stand silent & invisible,
tiny horses graze on the rusty canyon's mesquite floor.
At Mesa, on the car radio passing a new corn silo,
Walking Boogie teenager's tender throats, "I wish they
could all be California girls"—as black highway curls out-
ward.
On plains toward Pasco, Oregon hills at horizon, Bob
Dylan's voice on airways, mass machine-made folksong of
one soul—*Please crawl out your window*—first time heard.
Speeding thru space, Radio the soul of the nation.
The Eve of Destruction and The Universal Soldier.
And tasted the Snake: water from Yellowstone un-
der a green bridge; darshan with the Columbia, oilslick &
small bird feathers on mud shore. Across the river, silver

bubbles of refineries.

There Lewis and Clark floated down in a raft: the brown-mesa'd gorge of Lake Wallula smelling of rain in the sage, Greyhound buses speeding by.

Searching neither for Northwest Passage, nor Gold, nor the Prophet who will save the polluted Nation, nor for Guru walking the silver waters behind McNary Dam.

Round-up time in Pendleton, pinched women's faces and hulking cowboy hats in the tavern, I'm a city slicker from Benares. Barman murmurs to himself, two hands full of beer, "Who wanted that?"

Heavy rain at twilight, trumpets massing & ascending repeat The Eve of Destruction, Georgia-Pacific sawmill burners lifting smoke thru the dusky valley.

Cold night in Blue Mountains, snow-powdered tops of droopy Tamarack and Fir at grey sunrise, coffee frozen in brown coffeepot, toes chilled in Czechoslovakian tennis sneakers.

Under Ponderosa pine, this place for sale—45th Parallel, half way between equator and North Pole—Tri-City Radio broadcasting clear skies & freezing nite temperatures; big yellow daisies, hay bales piled in square stacks house-high.

"Don Carpenter has a real geologist's hammer, he can hit a rock & split it open & look inside & utter some mantra."

Coyote jumping in front of the truck, & down bank, jumping thru river, running up field to wooded hillside, stopped on a bound & turned round to stare at us—Oh-Ow! shook himself and bounded away waving his bushy tail.

Rifles & cyanide bombs unavailing—he looked real surprised & pointed his thin nose in our direction. Hari Om Namo Shivaye!

Eat all sort of things & run solitary—3 nites ago

hung bear dung on a tree and laughed

—Bear: "Are you eating my corpses? Say that again!"

Coyote: "I didn't say nothing."

Sparse juniper forests on dry lavender hills, down Ritter Butte to Pass Creek, a pot dream recounted:—Crossing Canada border with a tin can in the glove compartment, hip young border guards laughing—In meadow the skeleton of an old car settled: Look To Jesus painted on door.

Fox in the valley, road markers dript with small icicles, all windows on the white church broken, brown wooden barns leaned together, thin snow on gas station roof.

Malheur, Malheur National Forest—signs glazed snowfrost, last night's frozen dreams come back—staring out thru skull at cold planet—Mila-Repa accepted no gifts to cover his jewelled penis—Strawberry Mountain top white under bright clouds.

Postcards of Painted Hills, fossil beds near Dayville, Where have all the flowers gone? flowers gone? Ra and Coyote are hip to it all, nailed footpaw tracks on Day River bottom, cows kneeled at rest in meadow afternoon.

Ichor Motel, white tailfins in driveway, isolate belfried brown farmhouse circled with trees, chain saws ringing in the vale.

Rilled lava overgrown with green moss cracked in cold wind—Blue Heron and American white egret migrate to shrunken waters of Unhappy—mirage lakes wrongside of the road, dust streaming under Riddle Mountain, Steen Range powder white on horizon —

Slept, water froze in Sierra cup, a lake of bitter water from solar plexus to throat—Dreamt my knee was severed at hip and sutured back together —

Woke, icy dew on poncho and saffron sleep bag,

moon like a Coleman lantern dimming icicle-point stars—
vomited on knees in arroyo grass, nostrils choking with
wet red acid in weak flashlight —

Dawn weakness, climbing worn lava walls following
the muddy spring, waterfowl whistling sweetly & a tiny
raccoon

pawed forward daintly in green mud, looking for
frogs burrowed away from Arctic cold—disappeared into a
silent rock shelf.

Climbed up toward Massacre Lake road—sagebrush
valley-floor stretched South—Pronghorn abode, that eat
the bitter-root and dry spicebush, hunters gathering in
trucks to chase antelope —

A broken corral at highway hill bottom, wreck of a
dead cow in cold slanting sun set rays, eyes eaten out, neck
twisted to ground, belly caved on kneebone, smell of sweet
dread flesh and acrid new sage.

Slept in rusty tin feeding trough, Orion belt crystal
in sky, numb metal-chill at my back, ravens settled on the
cow when sun warmed my feet.

Up hills following trailer dust clouds, green shotgun
shells & beer-bottles on road, mashed jackrabbits—through
a crack in the Granite Range, an alkali sea—Chinese armies
massed at the borders of India.

Mud plate of Black Rock Desert passing, Frank
Sinatra lamenting distant years, old sad voic'd September'd
recordings, and Beatles crying Help! their voices woodling
for tenderness.

All memory at once present time returning, vast dry
forests afire in California, U.S. paratroopers attacking guer-
rillas in Vietnam mountains, over porcelain-white road
hump the tranquil azure of a vast lake.

Pyramid rocks knotted by pleistocene rivers, top-
heavy lava isles castled in Paiute water, cutthroat trout;
tomato sandwiches and silence.

Reno's Motel traffic signs low mountains walling the desert oasis, radio crooning city music afternoon news, Red Chinese Ultimatum 1 AM tomorrow.

Up Donner Pass over concrete bridge superhighways hung with grey clouds, Mongolian Idiot chow-yuk the laughable menu this party arrived.

Ponderosa hillsides cut back for railroad track, I have nothing to do, laughing over Sierra top, gliding adventurer on the great fishtail iron-finned road, Heaven is renounced, Dharma no Path, no Saddhana to fear,

my man world will blow up, humming insects under wheel sing my own death rasping migrations of mercy, I tickle the Bodhisattva and salute the new sunset, home riding home to old city on ocean

with new mantra to manifest Removal of Disaster from my self, autumn brushfire's smoky mass in dusk light, sun's bright red ball on horizon purple with earth-cloud, chanting to Shiva in the car-cabin.

Pacific Gas high voltage antennae trailing thin wires across flatlands, entering Coast Range 4 lane highway over last hump to giant orange Bay glimpse, Dylan ends his song "You'd see what a drag you are," and the Pope

cometh to Babylon to address United Nations, 2000 years since Christ's birth the prophecy of Armageddon

hangs the Hell Bomb over planet roads and cities, year-end come, Oakland Army Terminal lights burn green in evening darkness.

Treasure Island Naval Base lit yellow with night business, thousands of red tail lights move in procession over Bay Bridge,

San Francisco stands on modern hills, Broadway lights flash the center gay honky-tonk Elysium, Ferry building's sweet green clock lamps black Embarcadero waters, negroes screaming over radio,

Bank of America burns red signs beneath the neon

pyramids, here is the city, here is the face of war, home 8
o'clock
     gliding down freeway ramp to City Lights, Peter's
face and television, money and new wanderings to come.

September 1965

CONTINUATION OF A LONG POEM
OF THESE STATES:
S.F. Southward

Stage-lit streets
        Downtown Frisco whizzing past, buildings
        ranked by Freeway balconies
                Bright Johnny Walker neon
                        sign Christmastrees
And Christmas and its eves
        in the midst of the same deep wood
                as every sad Christmas before, surrounded
                        by forests of stars—
Metal columns, smoke pouring cloudward,
                yellow-lamp horizon
                        warplants move, tiny
                planes lie in Avionic fields —
Meanwhile Working Girls sort mail into the red slot
        Rivers of newsprint to soldiers' Vietnam
        Infantry Journal, Kanackee
                Social Register, Wichita Star
And Postoffice Christmas the same brown place
                mailhandlers' black fingers
                dusty mailbags filled
                        1948 N.Y. Eighth Avenue was
        or when Peter drove the mailtruck 1955
                        from Rincon Annex —
Bright lights' windshield flash,
                adrenalin shiver in shoulders
                        Around the curve
                crawling a long truck
                        3 bright green signals on forehead
        Jewelled Bayshore passing the Coast Range

          one architect's house light on hill crest
. . . . negro voices rejoice over radio
    Moonlight sticks of tea
Moss Landing Power Plant
     shooting its cannon smoke
         across the highway, Red tailight
         speeding the white line and a mile away
    Orion's muzzle
           raised up
               to the center of Heaven.

December 18, 1965

THESE STATES, INTO L.A.

Organs and War News
     Radio static from Saigon
          "And the Glory of the Lord"
          Newscaster Voice
           thru Aether —
The Truce —
     12 hours, 30 hours?
          Thirty Days, said Mansfield.
   Cars roll right lane,
     bridge lights
          rising & falling on night-slope —
     headlights cross speeding reflectors
Handel rejoicing
     chorus whine Requiem, roar in yr Auto
          window shoulders
Memories of Christmas —
     and the deep Christmas begins:
          U.S. 101 South
The President at home
     in his swinging chair on the porch
          listening to Christmas Carols
     Vice-President returning from Far East
"Check into yourself that you are wrong —
     You may be the Wrong" says Pope His
          Christmas Message —
Overpopulation, overpopulation
     Give me 3 acres of land
     Give my brother how much?
          Each man have fine estate?
          settle giant Communes?
LSD Shakti-snake settles like gas into Consciousness

       —Brightest Venus I've ever seen
Canyon-floor road, near
     bursting tides
  & caves they'd slept in earlier years
        covered with green water
        height of a man.
  A stranger walked that ground.
      Five years ago we picnicked
         in this place.
Auto track by a mud log, Bixby Creek
  wove channels
      thru the shifting sands.
I saw the ghost of Neal
      pass by, Ferlinghetti's ghost
  The ghost of Homer roaring at the surf
     barking & wagging his tail
  My own footprint at the sea's lips
     white foam to the rock where I sang
        Harekrishna
sand garden drying, kelp
    standing head upward in sunlight.
       Dinosaur hard, scabrous
   overgrown with seaweed tendrils,
       Professors of rock . . .

Where's Stravinsky? Theda Bara? Chaplin? Harpo Marx?
  Where's Laurel and his Hardy?
      Laughing phantoms
      going to the grave —
Last time this town   I saw them in movies
   Ending *The Road to Utopia* 'O Carib Isle!'
   Laurel aged & white-haired Hardy
      Hydrogen Comic smoke billowing
       up from their Kingdom —

Graumann's Chinese Theater's drab sidewalk front's
    concrete footprints, stood there
        stupid, anal, exciting
             upside down, Crosseyed moviestar'd
I craned at Myrna Loy & Shirley Temple shoe-marks —

Raccoon crouched at road-edge, praying —
                Carlights pass —
Merry Christmas to Mr. & Mrs.
            Chiang Kai Shek
Merry Christmas to President Johnson & pray for Health
Merry Christmas to MacNamara, State Secretary Rusk,
           Krushchev hid in his apartment house,
               to Kosygin's name, to Ho Chi Minh
                    grown old,
Merry Christmas to rosycheeked Mao Tze Tung
    Happy New Year Chou En Lai & Laurel and Hardy
Merry Christmas to the Pope
        & to the Dalai Lama Rebbe Lubovitcher
    to the highest Priests of Benin,
    to the Chiefs of the Faery Churches —
Merry Christmas to the Four Shankaracharyas,
    to all Naga Sadhus, Bauls & Chanting Dervishes
              from Egypt to Malaya —

Black Sign Los Angeles 140 Miles
    stifling car-heat —
        Music on the tacky radio,
           senseless, senseless coughs of emotion —
The Ally Cease-Fire Will Not Be Extended
            " . . . . . . on a densely populated area"
" . . .—Peking will never join the United Nations as long
as it remains under what it termed American Domination."

MOBILIZE THE NATIONAL GUARD, Sd/ Senator
                                    Anderson
        1Y Mental Rejectees will be reexamined
                    for service in Vietnam.
Bradley high on acid
        drawing pictures on Army Forms?
        Peter classified Psycho telling his Sergeant
            "An Army is an Army against Love."

Xmas day work   stack of papers on the President's desk
                            a foot high!
                        he has to finish them tonight!
    this determined NBC News entering Lompoc, famed of
                                    W.C. Fields
                who proved that Everyman's a
                                natural bullshit artist:
            "spends about 75% of his time on Foreign Matters
                                        and is,
                    uh, very involved . . ."
                        "and all letters are answered."
WHAT no Xmas message from the
                Texas White House?
        The President must be very *down* —
    He's maintaining his communications networks
                    circling the Planet.
                Mambo canned music mush
                Ventura radio Xmas sound
                        Commercial announcements,
        Few minutes of live speech, little joy or thanksgiving,
no voice from Himalayas
                Good Cheer Happy Kalpa
    for Dominica Vietnam Congo China India America
                Tho England rang with the Beatles!

    "healing all that was oppressed with the Devil."
  & at Santa Barbara exit
     the Preacher hollered in tongues
     YOUR NAME IS WRITTEN IN HEAVEN
       passing 38th Parallel
Lodge spoke from Saigon "We are morally right,
  we are Morally Right,
   serving the cause of freedom forever giving these
          people
    an opportunity . . . almost like thinking" —
 He's broadcasting serious-voice on Xmas Eve to America
Entering Los Angeles space age
  three stations simultaneous radio —
    Cut-Up Sounds that fill Aether,
      voices back of the brain —
    The voice of Lodge, all well, Moral —
    voice of a poor poverty worker,
      "Well they dont know anybody dont
      know anything about the poor all
      the money's going to the politicians
      in Syracuse, none of it's going
        to the poor."
    Evers' voice the black Christmas March
    "We want to be treated like Men,
      like human . . ."
  Mass Arrest of Campers Outside LBJ Ranch
Aquamarine lights revolving along the highway,
    night stars over L.A., exit trees,
 turquoise brilliance shining on sidestreets —

         Xmas Eve 1965

HIWAY POESY LA-ALBUQUERQUE-TEXAS-WICHITA

up up and away!
   we're off, Thru America —

Heading East to San Berdoo
   as West did, Nathaniel,
California Radio Lady's voice
   Talking about Viet Cong —
   Oh what a beautiful morning
   Sung for us by Nelson Eddy

Two trailor trucks, Sunkist oranges/bright colored
   piled over the sides
  rolling on the road —
Grey hulk of Mt. Baldy under
  white misted skies
Red Square signs unfold, Texaco Shell
   Harvey House tilted over the superhighway —

Afternoon Light
   Children in back of a car
   with Bubblegum
a flight of birds out of a dry field like mosquitos

". . . several battalions of U.S. troops in a search and
destroy operation in the Coastal plain near Bong Son, 300
mi. Northeast of Saigon. Thus far the fighting has been a
series of small clashes. In a related action 25 miles to the
South, Korean troops killed 35 Vietcong near Coastal
highway Number One."

"For he's oh so Good
and he's oh so fine
and he's oh so healthy
in his body and his mind"
                        The Kinks on car radio

In Riverside,
        a 1920's song —
            "It's the only words I know/that you'll
                                        understand"
        For my uncle Max dead 5 years ago
            it's settled—buried
under the blue mountain wall,
Veined with snow at the top
            clouds passing
                icy remote heights
Palmtrees on valleyfloor
    stick up toothpick hairheads —
Toy automobiles piled crushed and mangled
            topped by a hanging crane,
    The planet hanging,
            the air hanging,
                Trees hang their branches,
            A dirt truck hanging on the highway —
Spectacle of Afternoon,
        giant pipes glistening in the universe
    Magic that weighs tons and tons,
            Old bum with his rough
                tattered pack hunched
    walking up the hill hanging
                to Ukipah
            cloth cap pulled over his head
                        black fingernails.

    A wall, a wall, a Mesa Wall, There's desert
    flat mountain shadows

              miles along the pale pink floor:
                              —Indio in space.

The breath of spring, the breath of fear
              Mexican border . . .
                        The LSD cube —
                              silence.
There's those Hellies again,
              over hiway, as over Mekong
                        belly lights blinking red
              prob'ly surveying the border —
              shotguns stickin' out all over
                        —Two birds swoop under car dashboard.
                        Purple Mist,
                              motor tire drone.
Sacrifice for Prosperity, says Johnson.
        Joshua Tree Monument
Blue dusk.
              Bomb China
        says Southern Senator Stennis —
Mobil's neon Pegasus flying overhill.

Colorado River border,
        Two lemons an orange seized,
                  Scaley Mites
        and the cube of acid smuggled into Arizona . . .

"It all comes from Crystal hill" —
        The whole countryside's Quartzite hereabouts —
Huntley's Perspective on the News
              Sukarno a Nut? A wildman?
                  or potential friend?
        Brought to you by Mercury

boasting "sweet
success taste" —
They can go around saying things about people,
    and once their policy's adopted it'll rule a decade —
Somebody decided "he's a nut!"
        official policy, re-echoed to 14 Million Readers of
                                    Time
as we drive along in the Bat-mobile thru Arizona —
Approaching Hope, dream maps unfolded
                    Waves with larger & larger loops,
                    Tree-posts flashing auto headlights
                                    hit my retina
                    I saw what it was
                        light saw light,
                                    a flash in the pan.
Eyes register, nerves send waves along to the brain
Finger touch is electric waves
                    carlights glare thru eyes —
Voice repeating itself,
        wavering over the microphones —
                Meditation passing Hope . . .

Horrific outskirts' Eastern Traffic Sign,
        Turn backward . . .
                Dull sleep on my eyes
    *   *   *   *

Morning *Phoenix Gazette,* editorial January 27, '66
            "No time for probe of CIA
            No Good Purpose would be served —
                    Why poke on the Nose?
        . . . Virtual epidemic of attacks,
Pacifists let Reds take over the world, rather than
                    Fighting Against Them —
        well meaning people . . . distasteful intelligence

Sacrosanct...scuttle...demand an investigation ...
Where the spirit of the Lord is, there is liberty."
Righto! The Navaho trail —
Crescent moon setting on low hills West —
Military forces over radio
push bombing N. Vietnam.
Lifelines, sponsored by Henry L. Hunt, Beans.
Dead voiced announcer, denouncing
"a communist conspiracy among the youth ...
speakers on campuses/trained to condition
idealistic brains..."
It's Chase Manhattan Bank lends money to South African
White government—Rockefeller boy!
Unless Chase Bank quits I prophesy blood violence.
Ford has a factory,
Ford has a factory there —
"they're aw-fly proud
of being South African."
"...A hotbed of anti Semitism too?"

PAINTED DESERT,
petrified forest
Leslie Howard's scratchy '30s image
...eating jurassic steak
Petroglyphs over there the Man in the Moon,
the guy with four fingers...
over there, this is the sun, with two spikes out
the North,
two spikes South, two spikes ray East & West

Milky way over here, the Moon,
. . .and all the animal tentacles
Nebula spiraled   ". . . Roger 1943"
And I hit Julius for eating his avocado cheese sandwich
                                        too fast.

Gas flares, oil refinery night smoke,
high aluminum tubes winking red lights
                        over space ship runways
petrochemical witches' blood boiling underground —
"Looks like they're getten ready to go to Mars."
Approaching Thoreau —
                Fort Wingate Army Depot entrance —
                and there's the Continental Divide.
Anti Vietnam War Demonstrator soldiers sentenced
            For Contempt of President:
                        Hard Labor —
Learn theyself in Shell Refinery's Oil Storage
                        Seaboard Rackets,

Lying back on the car seat,
        eyelids heavy,
                legs spread leaned against the table,
Oh that I were young again and the skin in my anus folds
                                        rose,
    "La Illaha El L'Ill Allah Hu"
Finally bored,
        Over a hill, singing *Raghupati Raghava Raja Ram*
Albuquerque Sparkling blue brilliant
        more diamonds & pearls of electricity
        running out of power-plants than ever heard of
                Turkey or Israel —
intense endless iridescence on black
                velvet desert —
                Ah what a marvel

orange blue Neon Circling itself Solar System'd
Speed Wash Texaco 19¢ Famous Hamburgers
Lion House Italian Village Pizza ah!
radio warbles Electronic noise
      echo chamber vibrations —
          Albuquerque streets' fantastic Neon Stars
            collapsing to bright red blinks
Satellite Globes plunging their
                tiny lamps in and out —
                  the eyeball.

      *   *   *

Space stretching North dotted with silver gastanks
      to Sandia Range
Hitchhiking student
      supported by National Defense Fund
          with his black horn rimmed glasses,
             thin blond hair,
"If your country calls you, would you go?"
"If my country drafted me. . .
          then I would go."
Selfish young american always interested in his own skin
—and blue car speeding along the highway
      sticker on back
          "I'm proud I'm an American"
      right front seat, a 10 gallon hat
      driver a fat car salesman —
Sitting icy tipped
      distant earth peaks over Hilltops
& here's an ugly little oasis, used car tractors
          fenced off by barbed wire
            below roadside —
Evenings cool clear, sharp
          brilliant blue stars —
Just what we needed, State Penitentiary!

Two miles off into the brown furze rolling
East of the highway
"This is Ford Country what are *you* driving," Be a Ford
dealer?
Great snow meadows roof Sangre De Cristo
clouds, North, dipping misty rivulet tails of pointy fog.
. . . .
It's a hard question. . .
which would you rescue, your mother-in-law
or the last text of Shakespeare?
☆   ☆   ☆
Two hitchhikers, one Cajun dumb mouth
who sang brown voiced
blues his travellin' baby.
'Tother highschool smart
wavy hair, unbeautiful, unbeautiful
and gentle
pinched pachuco face
had ideas of his own philosophy —
thumbing out of Albuquerque
To New Orleans Mardigras
$900 a week, working rolling drunks, or
fixin signs with ladders and hammers
had spent 3 youth years in Siam,
Champagne & Pussy 50¢
kindly eyes
"I love to eat, and I love girls."
Sang them Prajnaparamita Sutra
entering Panhandle,
left them back at Tukumkarie —
talking in the truckstop booth,
fat truck drivers
headed south.

On Radio entering Texas
  Please For Jesus!
  Grunts & Screams & Shouts,
    Shouts for the Poison Redeemer,
  Shouts for the Venomous Jesus of Kansas.
Onward to Wichita!
  Onward to the Vortex!
    To the Birchite Hate Riddles,
   cock-detesting, pussy-smearing
   dry ladies and evil Police
     of Central Plains' State
  Where boredom & fury
    magick bars and sirens around
     the innocent citykid eye
 & Vampire stake of politics Patriotism's driven
  into the white breast of Teenage
   joyful murmurers
   in carpet livingrooms
    on sidestreets —
Beautiful children've been driven from Wichita
McClure & Branaman gone
  J. Richard White departed left no address
Charlie Plymell come *Now* to San Francisco
  Ann Buchanan passing thru,
Bruce Conners took his joke to another coast —
  in time the *White Dove Review*
   fluttered up from Tulsa
Flatland entering Great Plains
    Evil gathers in Cities,
    Eye mouth newspapers
  Television concentrates its blue
   flicker of death in the frontal lobe —
  Police department sirens wail,
    The building Department inspector Negates
    What the Fire Department has failed to

burn down —
Students departing for Iowa & Chicago,
New York beckoning at the end of the stage —
While Soviets have made soft landing on the moon
Today, be it rock or dust?
Now's Solar System born anew?
Red lights, red lights at highway end,
glass reflectors,
there's no one On the Road.
". . .Don't know what will happen to the proud
American soldiers in Vietnam"
said Ex Ambassador Ex General Taylor —

In this great space, Murcheson & Hunt,
Texas millionaires
sit in Isolate skyscrapers
on flatland dotted with lights
or, from cities, isolate from fairies
and screaming european dowagers & sopranos,
plot conspiracies against Communists,
send messages to New York, Austin, Wichita
Vancouver, Seattle, to Los Angeles —
Radio programs about the Federal Octopus —
Seraphs of Money Power on Texas plains
huge fat-bellied power-men
shoving piles of Capital
by train
across grasslands —
Shoving messages into myriad innocent-cleaned ears
Spiritual messages about spiritual war —
Come to Jesus
where the money is!
Texas voice

singing Vietnam Blues
Twanging
"I don't like to die/ a man I ain't about t' crawl"
In Vital-heart,
Big truck slowly lumbers through town —
Hotels raise signs, neon winks.
Liberal's the beginning of Kansas
Martial music filling airwaves—
only the last few weeks
waves of military music
drum taps drum beats trumpets
pulsing thru radiostations
not even sad,
bald Sopranos
Sacred Tenors from 1920's
Singing antique music style
What Patriot wrote that shit?
Something to drive out the Indian
Vibrato of Buffie St. Marie?
Doom call of McGuire?
The heavenly echo of Dylan's despair
before the silver microphone
in his snake suit,
a reptile boy
disappearing in Time —
soft shoe dancing on the Moon?
It'll be a relief when the Chinese take over Texas!
Lifeline pumping its venom "Communist
Conspiracy"
Secret documents Infiltrate & smash Vatican
broadcast to these empty plains,
Isolate farmhouses with radios
hearing the Horror Syndicate
take over the Universe!

Radiostations whistling & crashing against each other
                              on autoradio —
Full moonlight on blue snow
Loudspeaker blasting midnite static
                thru some European Swansong,
        Dit dat dits of outerspace communication
                blanking out Ear's substance
Vatican whistles undertone
        bloops and eeeeeps, trillion-antennae'd
            grid of the Shabda
If it's silent it isn't there —

            *   *   *   *

Entering Kansas
        little red towers blink distance,
                Lifeline, continued over 7 stations —
H.L. Hunt his books read,
                Cold reasoning voice over Kansas plains —
O that's Liberal Spread before us!
Truck stopped by roadside Weighing Station
                    *

Heavy Jewish voice heard over Kansas Radio
            Varning the Jews, Take safety in Christ
                —Dr. Michaelson
                and the Hebrew-Christian Hour
                    —P.O.B. 707 Los Angeles 53 —

In 1866 & 1881 the Carbon Companies paid
$2,500,000 for the bones of Buffalos
        Representing 31,000,000 Buffalos.
Handful of Buffalo, lightbrown back shining in the sun
        Grazing at the edge of River Ginnesca —
Peter says Oooo! What
                visions they must have of human beings —

       silent tolerant, head bent,
              cropping grass —
'Right now they're trying to take the Indian territories
              away, near Hopiland.
     Wanna build subdivisions,
              Mineral rights —
     The last lands of the redskins —
Saw it in the paper t'other day
       on the Highway near Tucson —'

Blue morning in Kansas,
     black lambs dotted in snow
     Ice gleaming in brown grass at roadside
       Corn stacks, small
       lined up around tree groves —
Kingman Salvage, rusty autos under rusty hill,
Jodrell Bank reporting Sensational pictures Rocks on the
                  Moon,
     "it's a hard surface —"

     information about Hog Scallops at Birth,
   Meat prices, Grain prices
   Steer Meat Dollar values,
     Appeal to end Property Tax

   Green signs,
     Welcome to Wichita
     Population 280,000

Jan. 28-29, 1966

AUTO POESY:
ON THE LAM FROM BLOOMINGTON

Setting out East on rain bright highways
            Indianapolis, police cars speeding past
            gas station—Stopped for matches
PLOWL of Silence,
      Street bulbs flash cosmic blue—darkness!
            POW, lights flash on again!
                  pavement-gleam
                  Mobil station pumps lit in rain
ZAP, darkness, highway power failure
            rain hiss
                  traffic lights dead black —
Ho! Dimethyl Triptamine flashing circle vibrations
            center Spiked —
            Einsteinian Mandala,
   Spectrum translucent,
. . . Television eyeball dots in treehouse Ken Kesey's
Power failure inside the head,
      neural apparatus crackling —
So drift months later past
                  Eli Lilly pharmaceuticals' tower walls
            asleep in early morning dark outside Indianapolis
Street lamps lit humped along downtown Greenfield
News from Dallas, Dirksen declareth
      "Vietnam Protesters have forgotten the lessons of
                                    History"

Across Ohio River, noon
      old wire bridge, auto graveyards,
      Washington town covered with rust—hm —

Feb '66

KANSAS CITY TO SAINT LOUIS

Leaving K.C. Mo.   past Independence   past Liberty
Charlie Plymell's memories of K.C. renewed
                    The Jewel-box Review,
                        white-wigged fat camps yakking abt
                        Georgie Washington and Harry T.
                filthier than any poetry reading I ever gave
                        applauded
            by the police negro wives Mafia subsidized

To East St. Louis on the broad road
                    Highway 70 crammed with trucks
            Last night almost broke my heart dancing to
                        Cant Get No Satisfaction
            lotsa beer & slept naked in the guest room —
                                            Now
Sunlit wooded hills overhanging the highway
rolling toward the Sex Factories of Indiana —
                    Automobile graveyard, red cars dumped
                    bleeding under empty skies —
            Birchfield's paintings, Walker Evans' photos,
                a white Victorian house on a hill —
Trumble & Bung of chamber music
                    pianoesque on radio — midwest culture
                        before rock and roll

If I knew   twenty years ago   what I know now
I coulda led a symphony orchestra in Minneapolis
                            & worn a tuxedo

Heart to heart, the Kansas voice of Ella Mae

"are you afraid of growing old,
afraid you'll no longer be attractive to your husband?"
". . . I dont see any reason" says the radio
"for those agitators —
Why dont they move in with the negroes? We've been
separated all along, why change things now? But I'll hang
up, some other Martian might want to call in, who has
another thought."
The Voice of Leavenworth
echoing thru space to the car dashboard
". . . causes and agitations, then, then they're doing the
work of the communists as J. Edgar Hoover says, and
many of these people are people with uh respectable,
bility, of a cloak of respectability that shows uh uh teach-
ers professors and students . . ."
hollow voice, a minister
breathing thru the telephone
"God created all the races . . . and it is only men who
tried to mix em up, and when they mix em up that's when
the trouble starts."

"No place like Booneville though, buddy" —
End of the Great Plains,
late afternoon sun, rusty leaves on trees
One of these days those boots will walk all over you

We the People — shelling the Vietcong
"Inflation has swept in upon us . . . Johnson administra-
tion rather than a prudent Budget . . . discipline the Ameri-
can people rather than discipline itself . . ."

I lay in bed naked in the guest room,
my mouth found his cock,
my hand under his behind
Till the whole body stiffened
and sperm choked my throat.

Michelle, John Lennon & Paul McCartney
      wooing the decade
          gaps from the 30s returned

Old earth rolling mile after mile patient
            The ground
              I roll on
                  the ground
           the music soars above
The ground electric arguments
           ray over
The ground dotted with signs for Dave's Eat Eat
      scarred by highways, eaten by voices
           Pete's Cafe —
                Golden land in setting sun
Missouri River icy brown, black cows,
      grass tufts standing up hairy on hills
              mirrored to heaven —
           Spring one month to come.
Sea shells on the ground strata'd by the turnpike —
          Old ocean evaporated away,
              Mastodons stomped, dinosaurs groaned
                when these brown hillocks were
              leafy steam-green-swamp-think
                    Marsh nations
    before the Birch Society was a gleam in the
                    Pterodactyl's eye
  —Aeroplane sinking groundward
      toward my white Volkswagen prehistoric
      white cockroach under high tension wires —
        my face, Rasputin in car mirror.

Funky barn, black hills approaching Fulton

where Churchill rang down the Curtain
                    on Consciousness
and set a chill which overspread the world
                one icy day in Missouri
                    not far from the Ozarks —
Provincial ears heard the Spenglerian Iron
                    Terror Pronouncement
            Magnificent Language, they said,
                    for country ears —
St Louis calling St Louis calling
        Twenty years ago,
                Thirty years ago
                        the Burroughs School
Pink cheeked Kenney with fine blond hair,
            his almond eyes aristocrat
                gazed,
            Morphy teaching English & Rimbaud
                at midnight to the fauns
        W.S.B. leather cheeked, sardonic
                waiting for change of consciousness,
                    unnamed in those days —
        coffee, vodka, night for needles,
                young bodies
                    beautiful unknown to themselves
                running around St Louis
        on a Friday evening
                getting drunk in awe & honor of the
                        terrific future these
red dry trees at sunset go thru two decades later
                They could've seen
        the animal branches, wrinkled to the sky
                & known the gnarled prophecy to come,
if they'd opened their eyes outa the whiskey-haze
                        in Mississippi riverfront bars
                and gone into the country with a knapsack to
                        smell the ground.

Oh grandfather maple and elm!
Antique leafy old oak of Kingdom City in the purple light
come down, year after year,
to the tune
of mellow pianos.
Salute, silent wise ones,
Cranking powers of the ground,
awkward arms of knowledge
reaching blind above the gas station
by the high TV antennae
Stay silent, ugly Teachers,
let me & the Radio yell about Vietnam and mustard gas.

"Torture . . . tear gas legitimate weapons . .
Worries language beyond my comprehension" the radio
commentator says himself.
Use the language today
". . . a great blunder"
in Vietnam, heavy voices,
"A great blunder . . . once you're in, uh,
one of these things, uh . . . "
"Stay in." Withdraw,
Language, language, uh, uh
from the mouths of Senators, uh
trying to think on their feet
Saying uhh, politely

Shift linguals, said Burroughs, *Cut the Word Lines!*
He was right all along.
". . . a procurer of these dogs
. . . take them from the United States . . . Major Caty . . .
as long as it's not a white dog . . . Sentry Dog Procurement
Center, Texas . . . No dogs, once trained, are ever returned
to the owner . . .

French Truth,
Dutch Civility
              Black asphalt, blue stars,
              tail light procession speeding East,
The hero surviving his own murder,
       his own suicide, his own
                     addiction, surviving his own
       poetry, surviving his own
                     disappearance from the scene —
returned in new faces, shining
       through the tears of new eyes.
              New small adolescent hands
                     on tiny breasts,
              pale silken skin at the thighs,
                     and the cherry-prick raises hard
                            innocent heat pointed up
                            from the muscular belly
of basketball highschool English class spiritual Victory,
       made clean at midnight in the bathtub of old City,
                            hair combed for love —
millionaire body from Clayton or spade queen from
                                   E St Louis
              laughing together in the TWA lounge
Blue-lit airfields into St Louis,
       past billboards ruddy neon,
              looking for old hero renewed,
                     a new decade —
Hill-wink of houses,
              Monotone road grey bridging the streets
              thin bones of aluminum sentinelled dark
              on the suburban hump bearing high wires
                            for thought to traverse
              river & wood, from hero to hero —

Crane all's well, the wanderer returns
                    from the west with his Powers,
        the Shaman with his beard
                    in full strength,
        the longhaired Crank with subtle humorous voice
                        enters city after city
            to kiss the eyes of your high school sailors
            and make laughing Blessing
                    for a new Age in America
    spaced with concrete but Souled by yourself
                    with Desire,
or like yourself of perfect Heart, adorable
            and adoring its own millioned population
                    one by one self-wakened
        under the radiant signs
            of Power stations stacked above the river
        highway spanning highway,
                    bridged from suburb to suburb.

March 1966

BAYONNE ENTERING NYC

Smog trucks mile after mile high wire
    Pylons trestled toward New York
        black multilane highway showered w/blue
                      arc-lamps,
        city glare horizoning
           Megalopolis with burning factories —
Bayonne refineries behind Newark Hell-light
    truck trains passing trans-continental gas-lines,
        blinking safety signs KEEP AWAKE
Giant giant giant transformers,
      electricity Stacks' glowing smoke —
    More Chimney fires than all Kansas in a mile,
Sulphur chemical Humble gigantic viaducts
              networked by road side
        What smell burning rubber, oil
            "freshens your mouth"
      Railroad rust, deep marsh garbage-fume
              Nostril horns —
    city Announcer jabbering at City Motel,
      flat winking space ships descending overhead
          GORNEY GORNEY MORTUARY
Brilliant signs the
    10 PM clock churchspire lit in Suburb City,
    New Jersey's colored streets asleep —
High derrick spotlites lamped an inch above
                roofcombs
      Shoprite lit for Nite people before the vast
  Hohokus marshes and Passaic's flat gluey
      Blackness ringed with lightbulbs.
Blue Newark airport, waiting for Uruguayan
          Ambassador's

        body arrive—green bulletshaped brain-
Plane, heartthrobbing redlight midriff
             settling down shark-swift
    toward the 71 million 3 hundred 69
      Lights at the field edge,
           Robot towers blazon'd Eastern Air TWA
          above the lavender bulbed runway
"Police say apparently had a heart attack—"
           Crossed barrage of car bridges —

I was born there in Newark
      Public Service sign of the 'Twenties
         visible miles away through smoke
             grey night over electric fields
My aunts and uncles died in hospitals,
      are buried in graves surrounded by Railroad Tracks,
        tombed near Winking 3 Ring Ballantine Ale's home
          where Western Electric has a Cosmic plant,
    Pitt-Consoles breathes forth fumes
        acrid above Flying Service tanks
      Where superhighway rises over Monsanto
           metal structures moonlit
      Pulaski Skyway hanging airy black
              in heaven my childhood
      neighbored with gigantic harbor stacks,
             steam everywhere
    Blue Star buses skimming skyroads
        beside th'antennae mazes
           brilliant by Canalside —

Empire State's orange shoulders lifted above the Hell,
New York City buildings glitter
          visible over Palisades' trees
        2 Guys From War put tiger in yr Tank —

Radio crawling with Rockmusic youngsters,
                    STOP—PAY TOLL.
let the hitchhiker off in the acrid Mist —
Blue uniformed attendants rocking on their heels
                            in green booths,
        Light parade everywhere
                Motel Hotel
                Lincoln Tunnel
                Pittsburg Shitsburg
                Seagram's A Sure One
                        Macdaniels vast parkinglot —
Cliff rooms, balconies & giant nineteenth
                        century schools,
    reptilian trucks on Jersey roads
Manhattan star-spread behind Ft. Lee cliffside
            Evening lights reflected across Hudson water —
brilliant diamond-lantern'd Tunnel
        Whizz of bus-trucks shimmer in Ear
                        over red brick
            under Whitmanic Yawp Harbor here
                roll into Man city, my city, Mannahatta
                    Lower East Side ghosted &
    grimed with Heroin, shit-black from Edison towers
                    on East River's rib —

Green-hatted doormen awaken the eve
                    in statuary-niched yellow lobbies —
    zephyrous canyons brightlit, grey stone Empire State
                    too small to be God
            lords it over sweet Macy's & Seafood City
                by junkey Grant Hotel —
Ho Ho turn right by the Blackman who crosses the street
            lighting his cigarette, lone on asphalt
                as the Lord in Nebraska —

Down 5th Avenue, brr—the irregular spine
of streetlights —
traffic signals all turned red at once —
insect lamps blink in dim artery
replicated down stone vales to Union Square —
In silence wait to see your home
Cemented asphalt, wire roof-banked,
canyoned, hived & churched with mortar,
mortised with art gas —
passing Ginsberg Machine Co.
th'axehead antique Flatiron
Building looms, old photographs
parked in the mind —
Canastra your 21st Street lofts dark no more raw
meat law business
Tonite Naomi your 18th Westside Stalinesque
madstreet's blocked by a bus,
Dusty your 16th (drunk in yr party dress) walls
emptiness   Hudson River perspectiv'd
Dali in London? Joe Army yr brokenbone Churches
stand brown in time —
How quiet Washington Monument!
& fairy youth turns head downstreet
crossing 5th Avenue under trafficlite,
doorman playing poodledog
on brilliant-lit sidewalk No. 1.
an old reporter w/ brown leather briefcase
leaves the shiny-pillared apartment —
Gee it's a Miracle to be back on this street
where strange guy mustache
stares in the windowshield —

Lovely the Steak Sign!   bleeps on & off
            beneath Woman's prison —
Sixth Avenue bus back-window bright glass
            Lady in kerchief leans backward,
corner Whalen's Drugs, an old Beret familiar face
            nods goodbye girl
Humm, Macdougal I lived here,
        Humm perfect, there's empty space
                Park by the bright-lit bookstore —
        Where I'll find my mail
            & Harmonium, new from Calcutta
Waiting I come back to New York & begin to Sing.

March 1966

II

Zigzag Back Thru These States

1966-1967

WINGS LIFTED OVER THE BLACK PIT

City Flats, Coal yards and brown rivers
      Tower groups toyed by silver bridge
            Sudden the snake uncoils
  w/ thousands of little bodies riding granite scales
  looped in approach to Geo. Washington's steel
                                trestle
          roped to Jersey west
  Blue sunray on air heights, bubbled with thick steam
                    roofing the planet —
      The jet plane glides toward Chicago.

Blue ground lands, chill cabin, white wings
      Stretch over mist-ribboned horizon
    small windows let in half moon
        a silver jet hangs in the sky south
    Brown gas of the City wrapped over hills —
Chanting Mantras all the way
    Hare Krishna etc
      Till dinner, great Lake below,
Heard a sweet drone in the plane-whine
    Hari Om Namo Shivaye— So
Made my own music
    American Mantra —
       "Peace in Chicago,
        Peace in Saigon—"
Raw orange sunset, & plunging in white cloud-shore
    Floated thru vast fog-waves
         down to black Chicago bottom

O'Hare Field's runway's blue insect lights on Wingèd
                                        Machinery
        Ozark Airways zoom up toward the Moon
Square Networks bulb-lit
        Twinkling blocks massed toward horizon
                        Kremlin'd with red towers,
        Aethereal cloverleafs' pinpointed circlets,
        Metropolis by night,
By air, Man's home filamented black panorama-skin
                brilliant below my chair & book —
        Impossible to be Mayor! know all details!?
        Alleyed with light,
                lampless yards
                        blazing compounds factoried cube-like,
                                prisons shining brilliant!
Suburban moviehouses' tiny glow
                by the Delicatessen corner,
        Vast hoards of men Negro'd in the gloom,
                gnashing their teeth for miles.
        Tears in attick's blackness
        Swastikas worshipped in the White Urb,
                clean teeth bared in Reptilian smiles —

Newsphoto Vision: M. L. King Attacked by Rocks —
Dark Land,
        Sparse networks of Serpent electricity
                Dotted between towers
        Signalling to themselves beneath the moon —

        ★   ★   ★   ★

Living like beasts,
        befouling our own nests,
                Smoke & Steam, broken glass & beer cans,

                              Auto exhaust —
Civilization shit littering the streets,
Fine black mist over apartments
            watercourses running with oil
               fish fellows dead —

                                        1966

CLEVELAND, THE FLATS

To D.A. Levy

Into the Flats, thru Cleveland's
                    Steeple trees illuminated
      Lake Bridge Light college cars speed round white lines
                  thru Green Lights, past downtown's pale Hotels
Triple towers smokestacked steaming in blue nite
                        buildings in water, the shimmer of that
                                    factory in the blackness
                      a little tinkle RR engine bell
See the orange bedroom shack
                    under the viaduct
crisscrossed with 1930's raindrops Tragedies
                      extrapolating railroads overhead —
          Asphalt road bumps —
                    that blue flame burning? Industry!
        Bom!   Bom! Mahadev! Microphone Icecream!
                          Battle Conditions! Come in Towers!
Buster Keaton died today, folksongs in the iron smell
                        of Republic Steel, hish—!
          American children crossing Jones Laughlin's yellow
                                  bridge saying o how
                  Beautiful, and Work ye Tarriers Work
                  in the fiery hill on the Press,
                        under black smoke —
Oh yes look, the lake mill lights —
                    Like an organpipe that smokestack
                            Hart Crane died under —

Black Tank Skeleton lifted over railroads' orange lamps,
illustrious robots stretched with wires,
     smoking organpipes of God in the Cleveland Flats
  Open hearth furnaces light up sky,
  all night gas station
Polack Stokers running out of money
   "Bearded short Amish, square-faced & incestuous,
    big-eared buck-toothed women, like crosseyed cats"
Steelton downhill, that smell What is it?
The guys wander up & down their gas refining Cracker
          climbing ladders in white light —
Butane smells—Creosote —
"Looka that gas-cloud we just passed thru—"
           Twin heavy smokestacks there —
Space age children wandering like lost orphans
    thru the landscape filled with iron —
     their grandfathers sweated over forges!
        now all they know is all them rockets they see
                    silvery
         Quivering on Television —
         I don't know any more.
Move ye wheels move
      for Independent Towel —
Dakota Hotel, old Red brick apartment,
up Carnegie to University Circle,
Om Om Om Sa Ra Wa Buddha Dakini Yea,
Benzo Wani Yea   Benzo Bero
   Tsani Yea Hūṃ Hūṃ Hūṃ
     Phat Phat Phat Svaha!

June 1966

A VOW

I will haunt these States
    with beard bald head
    eyes staring out plane window,
    hair hanging in Greyhound bus midnight
leaning over taxicab seat to admonish
    an angry cursing driver
    hand lifted to calm
    his outraged vehicle
that I pass with the Green Light of common law.

Common Sense, Common law, common tenderness
    & common tranquillity
our means in America to control the money munching
    war machine, bright lit industry
everywhere digesting forests & excreting soft pyramids
    of newsprint, Redwood and Ponderosa patriarchs
    silent in Meditation murdered & regurgitated as smoke,
    sawdust, screaming ceilings of Soap Opera,
    thick dead Lifes, slick Advertisements
    for Gubernatorial big guns
    burping Napalm on palm rice tropic greenery.

Dynamite in forests,
    boughs fly slow motion
    thunder down ravine,
    Helicopters roar over National Park, Mekong Swamp,
    Dynamite fire blasts thru Model Villages,
Violence screams at Police, Mayors get mad over radio,
    Drop the Bomb on Niggers!
    drop Fire on the gook China
    Frankenstein Dragon

waving its tail over Bayonne's domed Aluminum
oil reservoir!

I'll haunt these States all year
gazing bleakly out train windows, blue airfield
red TV network on evening plains,
decoding radar Provincial editorial paper message,
deciphering Iron Pipe laborers' curses as
clanging hammers they raise steamshovel claws
over Puerto Rican agony lawyers' screams in slums.

October 11, 1966

AUTUMN GOLD: NEW ENGLAND FALL

Auto Poetry to Hanover, New Hampshire

Coughing in the Morning
       Waking with a steam beast, city destroyed
       Pile drivers pounding down in rubble,
       Red smokestacks pouring chemical
                     into Manhattan's Nostrils — . . .
                   "All Aboard"
       Rust colored cliffs bulking over superhighway
                to New Haven,
       Rouged with Autumny leaves, october smoke,
           country liquor bells on the Radio —
Eat Meat and your a beast
       Smoke Nicotine & your meat'll multiply
          with tiny monsters of cancer,
Make Money & yr mind be lost in a million green papers,
    —Smell burning rubber by the steamshovel —
Mammals with planetary vision & long noses,
          riding a green small Volkswagen up three lane
               concrete road
                   past the graveyard
     dotted w/tiny american flags waved in breeze,
                     Washington Avenue:
Sampans battling in waters off Mekong Delta
   Cuban politicians in Moscow, analysing China —
Yellow leaves in the wood,
       Millions of redness,
         grey skies over sandstone
            outcroppings along the road —
cows by yellow corn,

      wheel-whine on granite,
          white houseroofs, Connecticut woods
            hanging under clouds —
Autumn again, you wouldn't know in the city
Gotta come out in a car see the birds
         flock by the yellow bush —
In Autumn, In autumn, this part of the planet's
        famous for red leaves —
Difficult for Man on earth to 'scape the snares of delusion —
   All wrong, the thought process screamed at
                   from Infancy,
The Self built with myriad thoughts
       from football to I Am That I Am,
Difficult to stop breathing factory smoke,
Difficult to step out of clothes,
      hard to forget the green parka —
Trees scream & drop
        bright Leaves,
Yea Trees scream & drop bright leaves,
Difficult to get out of bed in the morning
         in the slums —
Even sex happiness a long drawn-out scheme
        To keep the mind moving —

Big Grey truck rolling down highway
        to unload wares —
Bony white branches of birch relieved of their burden
—overpass, overpass, overpass
     crossing the road, more traffic
      between the cities,
         More sex carried near and far —
      Blinking tail lights
    To the Veterans hospital where we can all collapse,
Forget Pleasure and Ambition,

be tranquil and let leaves
blush, turned on
by the lightningbolt doctrine that rings
telephones
interrupting my pleasurable humiliating dream
in the locker room
last nite? —
Weeping Willow, what's your catastrophe?
Red Red oak, oh, what's your worry?
Hairy Mammal whaddya want,
What more than a little graveyard
near the lake by airport road,
Electric towers marching to Hartford,
Buildingtops spiked in sky,
asphalt factory cloverleafs spread over meadows
Smoke thru wires, Connecticut River concrete wall'd
past city central gastanks, glass boat bldgs.,
downtown, ten blocks square,
North, North on the highway, soon outa town,
green fields.
The body's a big beast,
The mind gets confused:
I thought I was my body the last 4 years,
and everytime I had a headache, God dealt me
Ace of Spades —
I thought I was mind-consciousness 10 yrs before that,
and everytime I went to the Dentist the Kosmos
disappeared,
Now I don't know who I am —
I wake up in the morning surrounded
by meat and wires,
pile drivers crashing thru the bedroom floor,
War images rayed thru Television apartments,
Machine chaos on Earth,
Too many bodies, mouths bleeding on every
Continent,

my own wall plaster cracked,
What kind of prophecy
for this Nation
Of Autumn leaves,
for those children in High School, green
woolen jackets
chasing football up & down field —
North of Long Meadow, Massachusetts
Shafts of Sunlight
Thru yellow millions,
blue light thru clouds,

President Johnson in a plane toward Hawaii,
Fighter Escort above & below
air roaring —
Radiostatic electric crackle from the
center of communications:
I broadcast thru Time,
He, with all his wires & wireless,
only an Instant —

Up Main Street Northhampton,
houses gabled sunny afternoon,
Ivy library porch —
Big fat pants, workshirt filled w/leaves,
painted pumpkinshead sitting Roof Corner,
— or hanging from frontyard tree country road —
Tape Machines, cigarettes, cinema, images,
Two Billion Hamburgers, Cognitive Thought,
Radiomusic, car itself,
this thoughtful Poet —
Interruption of brightly colored Autumn Afternoon,
clouds passed away —
Sky blue as a roadsign,

        but language intervenes.
              on route 9 going North —
"Then Die, my verse" Mayakovsky yelled
           Die like the rusty cars
                   piled up in the meadow —

Entering Whatley,
            Senses amazed on the hills,
           bright vegetable populations
               hueing rocks nameless yellow,
     veils of bright Maya over New England,
     Veil of Autumn leaves laid over the Land,
Transparent blue veil over senses,
               Language in the sky —
And in the city, brick veils,
     curtains of windows,
           Wall Street's stage drops,
     Honkeytonk scenery —
     or slum-building wall scrawled
         "Bourgeois Elements must go" —

All the cows gathered to the feed truck in the middle of
                        the pasture,
     shaking their tails, hungry for the yellow Fitten Ration
          that fills the belly
              and makes the eyes shine
                 & mouth go Mooooo.
Then they lie down in the hollow green meadow
                     to die —
In old Deerfield, Indian Tribes & Quakers
     have come & tried
            To conquer Maya-Time —
Thanksgiving pumpkins
     remain by the highway,
         signalling yearly Magic

                           plump from the ground.
Big leaves hang and hide the porch,
              & babies scatter by the red lights
                  of the bridge at Greenfield.
The green Eagle on a granite pillar —
             sign pointing route 2A The Mohawk Trail,
Federal Street apothecary shop & graveyard thru which
                  highschool athletes
                    tramp this afternoon —
Gold gold red gold yellow gold older than
                  painted cities,
      Gold over Connecticut River cliffs
      Gold by Iron railroad,
          gold running down riverbank,
      Gold in eye, gold on hills,
          golden trees surrounding the barn —
Silent tiny golden hills, Maya-Joy in Autumn
              Speeding 70 M.P.H.

October 17, 1966

DONE, FINISHED WITH THE BIGGEST COCK

Done, finished, with the biggest cock you ever saw.
3AM, living room filled with quiet yellow electric,
curtains hanging on New York, one window lit
in unfinished skyscraper.
                                            Swami White Beard
Being-Consciousness-Delight's photo's tacked
to bookshelf filled with Cosmic Milarepa, Wm. Blake's
Prophetic Writings, Buddhist Logic & Hymn to the Goddess,
and many another toy volume of orient lore, poetry crap;
Poe sober knew his white skull, tranquil Stein
repeated one simple idea *Making Americans* on Space Age's
edge whiten thought to transparent Place. Peace!
Done, finished with body cock desire, anger
shouting at bus drivers, Presidents & Police.
Gone to other shore, empty house, no lovers
suffering under bedsheets, inconceived babies calm.
Surge, a little abdomen warmth, the bus grinds
cobbles past red light, garbage trucks uplift iron
buttocks, old meat gravy & tin cans sink to bottom
in the Airfield. City edge woods wave branches
in chill breeze darkness under Christmas moon.

December 14, 1966

BAYONNE TURNPIKE TO TUSCARORA

Grey water tanks in Grey mist,
                              grey robot
        towers carrying wires thru Bayonne's
                        smog, silver
            domes, green chinaworks steaming,
            Christmas's leftover lights hanging
                              from a smokestack —
        Monotone grey highway into the grey West —
Noon hour, the planet smoke-covered
            Truck wheels roaring forward
                spinning past the garbagedump
        Gas smell wafting thru Rahway overpass
        oiltanks in frozen ponds, cranes' feederladders &
            Electric generator trestles, Batteries open under
                              heaven
Anger in the heart —
            hallucinations in the car cabin, rattling
            bone ghosts left and right
        by the car door—the broken icebox —
On to Pennsylvania turnpike
                              Evergreens in Snow
            Laundry hanging from the blue bungalow
Mansfield and U Thant ask halt Bombing North Vietnam
        State Department says "Tit For Tat."
                Frank Sinatra with negro voice
                        enters a new phase —
            Flat on his face 50 years "I've been a beggar & a
                              clown
                a poet & a star, roll myself in July
                        up into a ball and die."
                              Radio pumping

artificial rock & roll, Beach Boys
& Sinatra's daughter overdubbed microphone
antennae'd car dashboard vibrating
False emotions broadcast thru the Land
Natural voices made synthetic,
pflegm obliterated
Smart ones work with electronics —
What are the popular songs on the Hiway?
"Home I'm Comin Home I am a Soldier— "
"The girl I left behind . . .
I did the best job I could
Helping to keep our land free
I am a soldier"
Lulled into War
thus commercial jabber Rock & Roll Announcers
False False False
"Enjoy this meat—"
Weak A&P Superright ground round
Factories building, airwaves pushing . . .
Trees stretch up parallel into grey sky
Yellow trucks roll down lane —
Hypnosis of airwaves
In the house you can't break it
unless you turn off yr set
In the car it can drive yr eyes inward
from the snowy hill,
withdraw yr mind from the birch forest
make you forget the blue car in the ice,
Drive yr mind down Supermarket aisles
looking for cans of Save-Your-Money
Polishing-Glue
made of human bones manufactured in N. Vietnam
during a mustard gas hallucination:
The Super-Hit sound of All American Radio.

Turnpike to Tuscarora
      Snow fields, red lights blinking in the broken car
     Quiet hills' genital hair black in Sunset
     Beautiful dusk over human tinyness
          Pennsylvanian intimacy,
               approaching Tuscarora Tunnel
     Quiet moments off the road, Tussie Mountains'
              snowfields untouched.
A missile lost Unprogrammed
          Twisting in flight to crash 100 miles
            south of Cuba into the
              Blue Carib!
     Diplomatic messages exchanged
     "Don't Worry it's only the Setting Sun—"
     (Western correspondents assembling in Hanoi)
       "perfect ball of orange in its cup of clouds"
Dirty Snowbanks pushed aside from Asphalt thruway-edge —
Uphill's the little forests where the boyhoods grow
           their bare feet —

Night falling, "Jan 4 1967, The Vatican Announces Today
   No Jazz at the Altar!"
             Maybe in Africa
    maybe in Asia they got funny music
      & strange dancing before the Lord
   But here in the West No More Jazz at the Altar,
      "It's an alien custom—"
Missa Luba crashing thru airwaves with Demonic Drums
      behind Kyrie Eleison —
Millions of tiny silver Western crucifixes for sale
      in the Realms of King Badouin —
Color TV in this year—weekly
    the Pope sits in repose & slumbers to classical music

in his purple hat —
Gyalwa Karmapa sits in Rumtek Monastery Sikkim
& yearly shows his most remarkable woven
dakini-hair
black Magic Hat
Whose very sight is Total Salvation —
Ten miles from Gangtok—take a look!

* * * * *

Mary Garden dead in Aberdeen,
Jack Ruby dead in Dallas —
Sweet green incense in car cabin.
(Dakini sleeping head bowed, hair braided
over her Rudraksha beads
driving through Pennsylvania.
Julius, bearded, hasn't eaten all day
sitting forward, pursing his lips, calm.)
Sleep, sweet Ruby, sleep in America, Sleep
in Texas, sleep Jack from Chicago,
Friend of the Mafia, friend of the cops
friend of the dancing girls —
Under the viaduct near the book depot
Under the hospital Attacked by Motorcades,
Under Nightclubs under all the
groaning bodies of Dallas,
under their angry mouths
Sleep Jack Ruby, rest at last,
bouquet'd with cancer.
Ruby, Oswald, Kennedy gone
New Years' 1967 come,
Reynolds Metals up a Half
Mary Garden, 92, sleeping tonite in Aberdeen.

Three trucks adorned with yellow lights crawl uproad
under winter network-shade, bare trees, night fallen.

Under Tuscarora Mountain, long tunnel,
                    WBZ Boston coming thru —
          "Nobody needs icecream nobody *needs* pot nobody
                                        needs movies."
. . . "Public Discussion."
          Is sexual Intercourse any Good? Can the kids handle it?
                    out the Tunnel,
The Boston Voice returning: "controlled circumstances . . ."
                    Into tunnel, static silence,
               Trucks roar by in carbon-mist,
                         Anger falling asleep at the heart.
White Rembrandt, the hills —
          Silver domed silo standing above house
          in the white reality place:
                                   farm up the road,
     Mist Quiet on Woods,
          Silent Reality everywhere.
Till the eye catches the billboards —
          Howard Johnson's Silent Diamond Reality
          "makes the difference."
Student cannon fodder prepared for next Congress session
  Willow Hill, Willow hill, Cannon Fodder, Cannon fodder —
And the Children of the Warmakers're exempt from fighting
                    their parents' war —
Those with intellectual money capacities who go to college
                    till 1967 —
Slowly the radio war news
               steals o'er the senses —
     Negro photographs in Rochester
                         axe murders in Cleveland,
          Anger at heart base
               all over the Nation —

Husbands ready to murder their wives
            at the drop of a hat-statistic
        I could take an axe and split Peter's skull with
                                pleasure —
Great trucks crawl up road
                insect-lit with yellow bulbs outside Pittsburgh,
        "The Devil with Blue Dress" exudes over radio,
                car headlights gleam on motel signs in
                                        blackness,
                Satanic Selfs covering nature
                        spiked with trees.
Crash of machineguns, ring of locusts, airplane roar,
                calliope yell, bzzzs.

AN OPEN WINDOW ON CHICAGO

Midwinter night,
    Clark & Halstead brushed with this week's snow
    grill lights blinking at the corner
                decades ago
    Smokestack poked above roofs & watertower
        standing still above the blue
              lamped boulevards,
  sky blacker than th' east
    for all the steel smoke
              settled in heaven from South.
Downtown—like Batman's Gotham City
        battleshipped with Lights,
    towers winking under clouds,
      police cars blinking on Avenues,
          space above city misted w/ fine soot
cars crawling past redlites down Avenue,
            exuding white wintersmoke —
Eat Eat said the sign, so I went in the Spanish Diner
The girl at the counter, whose yellow Bouffant roots
    grew black over her pinch'd face,
    spooned her coffee with knuckles
        puncture-marked,
  whose midnight wrists had needletracks,
      scars inside her arms: —
"Wanna go get a Hotel Room with me?"
        The Heroin Whore
thirty years ago come haunting Chicago's midnite streets,
  me come here so late with my beard!

Corner Grill-lights blink, police car turned
    & took away its load of bum to jail,

          black uniforms patrolling streets
    where suffering
          lifts a hand palsied by Parkinson's Disease
                to beg a cigarette.

The psychiatrist came visiting this Hotel 12th floor —
      Where does the Anger come from?
          Outside! Radio messages, images on Television,
                      Electric Networks spread
                fear of murder on the streets —
                  "Communications Media"
inflict the Vietnam War & its anxiety on every private skin
          in hotel room or bus —
Sitting, meditating quietly on Great Space outside —
Bleep Bleep dit dat dit radio on, Television
                          murmuring,
          bombshells crash on flesh
            his flesh my flesh all the same—.
The Dakini in the hotel room turns in her sleep
                while War news flashes thru Aether —
      Shouts at streetcorners as bums
                crawl in the metal policevan.
And there's a tiny church in middle Chicago
                with its black spike to the black air
And there's the new Utensil Towers round on horizon.
And there's red glow of Central Neon
                on hushed building walls at 4 AM,
And there's proud Lights & Towers of Man's Central City
          looking pathetic at 4 AM, traveller passing through,
          staring outa hotel window under Heaven —
Is this tiny city the best we can do?
      These tiny reptilian towers
          so proud of their Executives
          they haveta build a big sign in middle downtown
                          to Advertise

old Connor's Insurance sign fading on brick
                              building side —
     Snow on deserted roofs & Parkinglots —
     Hog Butcher to the World!?
            Taxi-Harmonious Modernity grown rusty-old —
The prettiness of Existence! To sit at the window
         & moan over Chicago's stone & brick
              lifting itself vertical tenderly,
                    hanging from the sky.

Elbow on windowsill,
     I lean and muse, taller than any building here
Steam from my head
         wafting into the smog
         Elevators running up & down my leg
Couples copulating in hotelroom beds in my belly
                & bearing children in my heart,
         Eyes shining like warning-tower Lights,
             Hair hanging down like a black cloud —
Close your eyes on Chicago and be God,
         all Chicago is, is what you see —
That row of lights Finance Building
         sleeping on its bottom floors,
        Watchman stirring
      paper coffee cups by Bronzed glass doors —
and under the bridge, brown water
           floats great turds of ice beside buildings' feet
      in windy metropolis
               waiting for a Bomb.

Jan 8, 1967

RETURNING NORTH OF VORTEX

Red Guards battling country workers
          in Nanking
Ho-Tei trembles,
        Mao's death near,
Snow over Iowa
      cornstalks on icy hills,
bus wheels murmuring in afternoon brilliance toward
                                   Council Bluffs
      hogs in sunlight, dead rabbits on asphalt
      Booneville passed, Crane quiet,
      highway empty — silence as
house doors open, food on table,
                nobody home —
    sign thru windshield
    100 Miles More to the Missouri.
How toy-like Pall Mall's red embossed pack
      cellophane gleaming in sunshine,
           Indian-head stamped crown crested,
     shewing its dry leaf of history to my eye
now that I no longer reach my hand to the ashtray
        nor since Xmas have lit a smoke.
One puff I remember the 18 year joy-musk of manhood
      that curled thru my nostrils first time I kissed
           another human body —
      that time with Joe Army, he seduced me
              into smoking —
I'll give Swami a present like Santa Claus —
           no attachment —
    No meat nor tabaccy — even sex questionable
    Now in America craving its billions
             of needles of War.

Detach yrself from Matter, & look about
           at the bright snowy show of Iowa,
        Earth & heaven mirroring
            eachother's light,
     tiny meat-trucks rolling downhill
         toward deep Omaha.
This is History, to quit smoking Anger-leaf
       into one man's lungs,
       glancing up at gravestone rows
            in hill woods thru rear window.

This is History: Iowa's Finest Comics:
     Sunday, Rex Morgan M.D. in snowstorm,
     Mustachio'd villain cruel eyed
         with long European hair
           doubletalking the Doc
    "Meanwhile, under the influence of LSD
    Veronica races through the fields
       in an acute panic" —
     Author Dal Curtis
In a violet box her big tits fall on snowy ground.
Grey ice floating down Missouri, sunset into Omaha
Bishop's Buffets, German Chocolate, wall to wall carpet
        Om A Hah, Om Ah Hūṃ
"The land summoned them and they loved it" cut in granite
         Post Office lintel, Walt Disney
    playing at State week after his death.
      Table service, fireplace, armchairs,
        homeostasis in Omaha.

Steve Canyon Comics in Color:
     U.S. Military Seabees chopper
       operation dropping bridges
   over the "Lake of the Black Wind"

Princess Snowflower will
        "speak over the bullhorn to the
                 herdsmen —
        So they won't think it's a Chincom trick."
      Ten-year-olds in Sunday
         morning sunlight on the rug
    dreaming of slack-cheekboned blond
            big cocked Steve Canyon
               fucking the yellow bellies
   tied face down naked on the floor of the lone helicopter —
And on Sunday Evening the Reverend Preacher
        C.O. Staggerflup —
            America's Hope
        POB 72 Hopkins Minnesota
Isaiah denouncing the root of Evil to the Nation
14 billion 200 million a year to the Debt Money System,
           Rolling back darkness in Nebraska —
Shanghai water power cut off by Mao's enemies
       I am a Rock, I am an Island   radio souls cry
     passing north of Lincoln's tiny bright downtown horizon;
       Square banks huddled under Capitol turret blinking red
       electric tower steam-drifts
              ribboned across building tops
                 under city's ruby night-glow —
Let the Vietcong win over the American Army!
       Dice of Prophecy cast on the giant plains!
Drum march on airwaves, anger march in the mouth,
Xylophones & trumpets screaming thru American brain —
       Our violence unabated after a year
     in mid-America returned, I prophesy against
       this my own Nation

enraptured in hypnotic war.
And if it were my wish, we'd lose & our will
be broken
& our armies scattered as we've scattered the airy guerrillas
of our own yellow imagination.
Mothers weep & Sons be dumb
your brothers & children murder
the beautiful yellow bodies of Indochina
in dreams invented for your eyes by TV
all yr talk gibberish mouthed by radio,
yr politics mapped by paper Star
Thought Consciousness
Form Feeling Sensation Imagination the
5 skandas, realms of Buddha
Invaded by electronic media KLYL
News Bureau
& yr trapped in red winking Kansas
one giant delicate electrical antenna upraised
in midwinter Nebraska plains blackness
January 1967
I hope we lose this war.

Lincoln airforce Base, Ruby, Gochner
US 80 near Big Blue River,
The radio Bibl'd Hour, Dallas Texas
a great nose pushed out of the dashboard
demanding Your Faith Pledge!
Money your dollars support
The Radio Bible Hour.
You pledge to God to send
100 or 10 or 2 or $1 a month to the
Radio Bible Hour —
The electric network selling itself:
"The medium is the message"
Even so, Come, Lord Jesus!

Straight thru Nebraska at Midnight
        toward North Platte & Ogalalla
    returning down black superhighways to Denver.

January 8, 1967

KISS ASS

Kissass is the Part of Peace
America will have to Kissass Mother Earth
Whites have to Kissass Blacks, for Peace & Pleasure,
Only Pathway to Peace, Kissass.

Houston, Texas
24 April 1968

ELEGY CHÉ GUÉVARA

European Trib. boy's face photo'd eyes opened,
    young feminine beardless radiant kid
        lain back smiling looking upward
Calm as if ladies' lips were kissing invisible parts of the body
Aged reposeful angelic boy corpse,
      perceptive Argentine Doctor, petulant Cuba Major
            pipe mouth'd & faithfully keeping Diary
               in mosquitos Amazonas
Sleep on a hill, dull Havana Throne renounced
More sexy your neck than sad aging necks of Johnson
              DeGaulle, Kosygin,
    or the bullet pierced neck of John Kennedy
Eyes more intelligent glanced up to death newspapers
    Than worried living Congress Cameras passing
        dot screens into T.V. shade, glass-eyed
        MacNamara, Dulles in old life . . .

Women in bowler hats sitting in mud outskirts 11,000 feet
              up in Heaven
      with a headache in LaPaz
    selling black potatoes brought down from earth
             roof'd huts
     on mountain-lipped Puno
  would've adored your desire and kissed your Visage
           new Christ
  They'll raise up a red-bulb-eyed war-mask's

white tusks to scare soldier-ghosts
who shot thru your lungs

Incredible! one boy turned aside from operating room
or healing Pampas yellow eye
To face the stock rooms of ALCOA, Myriad Murderous
Board Directors of United Fruit
Smog-Manufacturing Trustees of Chicago U
Lawyer Phantoms ranged back to dead
John Foster Dulles' Sullivan & Cromwell Lawfirm
Acheson's mustache, Truman's bony hat
To go mad and hide in jungle on mule & point rifle at OAS
at Rusk's egoic Courtesies, the metal deployments of
Pentagon
derring-do Admen and dumbed intellectuals
from *Time* to the CIA
One boy against the Stock Market all Wall Street ascream
since Norris wrote *The Pit*
afraid of free dollars showering from the Observer's
Balcony
scattered by laughing younger brothers,
Against the Tin Company, against Wire Services,
against infra-red sensor Telepath Capitalism's
money-crazed scientists
against College boy millions watching Wichita Family
Den T.V.

One radiant face driven mad with a rifle
Confronting the electric networks.

Nov. 1967—Venice, Italy

WAR PROFIT LITANY

To Ezra Pound

These are the names of the companies that have made
    money from this war
nineteenhundredsixtyeight Annodomini fourthousand
    eighty Hebraic
These are the Corporations who have profited by merchan-
    dising skinburning phosphorus or shells fragmented
    to thousands of fleshpiercing needles
and here listed money millions gained by each combine for
    manufacture
and here are gains numbered, index'd swelling a decade, set
    in order,
here named the Fathers in office in these industries, tele-
    phones directing finance,
names of directors, makers of fates, and the names of the
    stockholders of these destined Aggregates,
and here are the names of their ambassadors to the Capital,
    representatives to legislature, those who sit drinking
    in hotel lobbies to persuade,
and separate listed, those who drop Amphetamines with
    military, gossip, argue, and persuade
suggesting policy naming language proposing strategy, this
    done for fee as ambassadors to Pentagon, consul-
    tants to military, paid by their industry:
and these are the names of the generals & captains mili-
    tary, who now thus work for war goods manufactur-
    ers;
and above these, listed, the names of the banks, combines,
    investment trusts that control these industries:
and these are the names of the newspapers owned by these

      banks
and these are the names of the airstations owned by these
      combines;
and these are the numbers of thousands of citizens em-
      ployed by these businesses named;
and the beginning of this accounting is 1958 and the end
      1968, that statistic be contained in orderly mind,
      coherent & definite,
and the first form of this litany begun first day December
      1967 furthers this poem of these States.

III

Elegies for Neal Cassady

1968

ELEGY FOR NEAL CASSADY

OK Neal
      aethereal Spirit
                  bright as moving air
                        blue as city dawn
happy as light   released by the Day
      over the city's new buildings —

Maya's Giant bricks rise rebuilt
                        in Lower East Side
   windows shine in milky smog.
            Appearance unnecessary now.

Peter sleeps alone next room, sad.
Are you reincarnate? Can ya hear me talkin?
If anyone had strength to hear the invisible,
And drive thru Maya Wall
      you *had* it —
                  What're you now, Spirit?
That were spirit in body —

The body's cremate
                  by Railroad track
            San Miguel Allende Desert,
                  outside town,
            Spirit become spirit,
                  or robot reduced to Ashes.

Tender Spirit, thank you for touching me with tender hands
When you were young, in a beautiful body,
      Such a pure touch it was Hope beyond Maya-meat,
      What you are now,

               Impersonal, tender —
you showed me your muscle/warmth/over twenty years ago
when I lay trembling at your breast
               put your arm around my neck,
—we stood together in a bare room on 103'd St.
Listening to a wooden Radio,
                     with our eyes closed
Eternal redness of Shabda
               lamped in our brains
at Illinois Jacquet's Saxophone Shuddering,
     prophetic Honk of Louis Jordan,
       Honeydrippers, Open The Door Richard
           To Christ's Apocalypse —
The buildings're insubstantial —
That's my New York Vision
              outside eastern apartment offices
     where telephone rang last night
             and stranger's friendly Denver Voice
asked me, had I heard the news from the West?

Some gathering Bust, Eugene Oregon or Hollywood Impends
           I had premonition.
"No" I said —"been away all week,"
       "you havent heard the News from the West,
            Neal Cassady is dead—"
     Peter's dove-voic'd Oh! on the other line, listening.

Your picture stares cheerful, tearful, strain'd,
             a candle burns,
      green stick incense by household gods.
Military Tyranny overtakes Universities, your Prophecy
     approaching its kindest sense brings us
                        Down
        to the Great Year's awakening.

Kesey's in Oregon writing novel language
                        family farm alone.
Hadja no more to do? Was your work all done?
        Had ya seen your first son?
                Why'dja leave us all here?
        Has the battle been won?

I'm a phantom skeleton with teeth, skull
        resting on a pillow
                calling your spirit
      god echo consciousness, murmuring
                sadly to myself.

Lament in dawnlight's not needed,
                    the world is released,
      desire fulfilled, your history over,
              story told, Karma resolved,
                      prayers completed
    vision manifest, new consciousness fulfilled,
               spirit returned in a circle,
world left standing empty, buses roaring through streets —
      garbage scattered on pavements galore —
Grandeur solidified, phantom-familiar fate
                returned to Auto-dawn,
                    your destiny fallen on RR track
My body breathes easy,
             I lie alone,
                    living
After friendship fades from flesh forms —
heavy happiness hangs in heart,
        I could talk to you forever,
              The pleasure inexhaustible,
                discourse of spirit to spirit,
                        O Spirit.

Sir spirit, forgive me my sins,
Sir spirit give me your blessing again,
Sir Spirit forgive my phantom body's demands,
Sir Spirit thanks for your kindness past,
Sir Spirit in Heaven, What difference was yr mortal form,
       What further this great show of Space?
      Speedy passions generations of
         Question? agonic Texas Nightrides?
         psychedelic bus hejira-jazz,
      Green auto poetries, inspired roads?
Sad, Jack in Lowell saw the phantom most —
      lonelier than all, except your noble Self.
Sir Spirit, an' I drift alone:
           Oh deep sigh.

10 Feb 1968 5-5:30 AM

CHICAGO TO SALT LAKE BY AIR

If Hanson Baldwin got a bullet in his brain, outrage?
If President Johnson got a bullet in his brain, fast Karma?
If *Reader's Digest* got a bullet in its brain would it be
    smarter?
March '68 P. 54 "Report from Vietnam, The foe is Hurt-
    ing"
. . . "The dismal picture of 1965, when I previously visited
    Vietnam,
has been reversed: The Allies are winning, and the enemy
    is being hurt,"
wrote *"The distinguished military Editor of the New York
    Times"*
The Dynosaur moves slowly over Chicago.
Arrived on United Airlines just in time all wrong.
Anger in the back of the plane cabin, anger at *Reader's
    Digest*
Hanson Baldwin's "Allies?" Hanson Baldwin's "The
    Enemy?"

Arguing with a schizophrenic is hopeless. A bullet in the
    brain.
Mr. Baldwin suggests more bullets in the brain to solve his
    Vietnam Problem.
Hanson Baldwin is a Military Ass-Kisser

Dead Neal was born in Salt Lake, & Jim Fitzpatrick's dead.
Flowers die, & flowers rise red petaled on the field.

Anger, red petal'd flower in my body

Detroit's lake from a mile above chemical muddy,
streams of grey waste fogging the surface to the center,
more than half the lake discolored metallic —
Cancerous reproductions the house flats rows of bee

boxes, DNA Molecular Patterns
microscopic reticulations topt w/ Television Antennae
and the horizon edged with grey gas clouds from East to
    West unmoved by wind.

They fucked up the planet! Hanson Baldwin Fucked up
    the Planet all by himself,
emitted a long Military gas cloud Dec 26 27 28 1967 in
    NY Times.
"Purely military considerations" he told TV —
Till Gov. LaSalle sd/ the Prexy cdnt be peaceful till elec-
    tion time,
as Baldwin nodded agree.

A bunch of fat & thin Schizophrenics running the planet
    thoughtwaves.

Shit, Violence, bullets in the brain Unavailing.
We're in it too deep to pull out.
Waiting for an orgasm, Mr. Baldwin?
Yes, waiting for an orgasm that's all.

Give 'em all the orgasms they want.
Give 'em orgasms, give Hanson Baldwin his lost orgasms.
Give *NY Times,* give *Reader's Digest* their old orgasms
    back.

It's a gold crisis! not enuf orgasms to go round
"I take care of other people's business" said th' old man
    sleeping next seat,
Wallets & pens in his inside pocket green tie black suit
    boots,
"Ever since the world began Gold is the measure of Soli-
    darity."
Golden light over Iowa, silver cloud floor, sky roof blue

deep
rayed by Western Sun set brightness from the center of the
    Solar System.
Neal born in Salt Lake. Died in San Miguel, met in Denver
    loved in Denver —
"Down in Denver/down in Denver/all I did was die."
                                              J. Kerouac, '48

Airplanes, a pain in the neck. Thru Heaven, a heavy roar,
vaportrails to the sun moving behind Utah's valley wall.
Give Heaven orgasms, give Krishna all your orgasms, give
    yr orgasms to the clouds. Great Salt Lake!
Fitzpatrick sobbed a lot in New York & Utah, his nervous
    frame racked with red eyed pain.
Farewell Sir Jim, in shiny heaven, bodiless as Neal's bodi-
    less . . .

Brainwash cried Romney, the Governor of Pollution,

Michigan's Lakes covered w/ green slime

> *"The people now see thru the Administration's con-*
> *tinuous brainwashing."*
> *Chi Trib* Mar 16. '68 A.P. Dispatch.

Mind is fragments . . . whatever you can remember from
    last year's *Time*
Magazine, this years sunset or grey cloudmass over
    Nebraska,
Leroi Jones' deep scar brown skin at left temple hair-
    line . . . .
. . . Don McNeil emerging from Grand Central w/6 stitches
    in Forehead

pushed thru plateglass by police, his presscard bloodied.

Deeper into grey clouds, there must be invisible farms,
     invisible farmers walking up and down rolling
     cloud-hills.
"A hole in its head" . . . another World, America, Viet
     Nam.
The Martians have holes in their head, like Moore's statu-
     ary.
& if Dolphin-like Saturnian tongues are invisible & their
     ecstatic language irrelevant to the Gold Supply
We'll murder 'em like 100,000,000 Bison —
Do the Buffalo Dance in the Jetplane over Nebraska! Bring
     back the Gay '90s.
Gobble gobble sd/ Sanders
& Turkeys' hormone-white-meat drumsticks poison the
     glands of suburban kiddies Thanksgiving.
On their bicycles w/ poison glands & DDT livers, halluci-
     nating Tiny Vietnams on TV.

Clouds rifts, Gold orgasms in the West,
Nebraska's Steppes herding broken cloud-flocks —
Sun at plane's nose, izzat the Missouri breaking the plains
     apart? Council Bluffs & Great Platte gone?
Oh Rockies already? Snow in granite cracks & grey crags.
Hanson Baldwin covered w/ Snowflakes.
Red oxide in air & earth, sunset flowers in clouds, Anger in
     the Heart,
"Croakers & doubters" . . . Napalm & Mace: Dogs!
Earth ripples, river snakes, iron horse tracks, car paths thin
—Wasatch peak snows, north crags' springtime white wall
     over desert-lake brightness —
Salt Lake streets at dusk flowing w/ electric gold. Beautiful
     Million winking lights!
Neal was born in Paradise!

March 30, 1968

MANHATTAN 'THIRTIES FLASH

Long stone streets inanimate, repetitive machine Crash
      cookie-cutting
dynamo rows of soulless replica Similitudes brooding
      tank-like in Army Depots
Exactly the same exactly the same exactly the same with
      no purpose but grimness
& overwhelming force of robot obsession, our slaves are
      not alive
& we become their sameness as they surround us—the long
      stone streets inanimate,
crowds of executive secretaries alighting from subway 8:30
      AM
bloodflow in cells thru elevator arteries & stairway glands
      to typewriter consciousness,
Con Ed skyscraper clock-head gleaming gold-lit at sun dusk.

1968

PLEASE MASTER

Please master can I touch your cheek
please master can I kneel at your feet
please master can I loosen your blue pants
please master can I gaze at your golden haired belly
please master can I gently take down your shorts
please master can I have your thighs bare to my eyes
please master can I take off my clothes below your chair
please master can I kiss your ankles and soul
please master can I touch lips to your hard muscle hairless
      thigh
please master can I lay my ear pressed to your stomach
please master can I wrap my arms around your white ass
please master can I lick your groin curled with blond soft
      fur
please master can I touch my tongue to your rosy asshole
please master may I pass my face to your balls,
please master, please look into my eyes,
please master order me down on the floor,
please master tell me to lick your thick shaft
please master put your rough hands on my bald hairy skull
please master press my mouth to your prick-heart
please master press my face into your belly, pull me slowly
      strong thumbed
till your dumb hardness fills my throat to the base
till I swallow & taste your delicate flesh-hot prick barrel
      veined Please
Master push my shoulders away and stare in my eye, &
      make me bend over the table
please master grab my thighs and lift my ass to your waist
please master your hand's rough stroke on my neck your
      palm down my backside

please master push me up, my feet on chairs, till my hole
    feels the breath of your spit and your thumb stroke
please master make me say Please Master Fuck me now
    Please
Master grease my balls and hairmouth with sweet vaselines
please master stroke your shaft with white creams
please master touch your cock head to my wrinkled self-
    hole
please master push it in gently, your elbows enwrapped
    round my breast
your arms passing down to my belly, my penis you touch
    w/ your fingers
please master shove it in me a little, a little, a little,
please master sink your droor thing down my behind
& please master make me wiggle my rear to eat up the
    prick trunk
till my asshalfs cuddle your thighs, my back bent over,
till I'm alone sticking out, your sword stuck throbbing in
    me
please master pull out and slowly roll into the bottom
please master lunge it again, and withdraw to the tip
please please master fuck me again with your self, please
    fuck me Please
Master drive down till it hurts me the softness the
Softness please master make love to my ass, give body to
    center, & fuck me for good like a girl,
tenderly clasp me please master I take me to thee,
& drive in my belly your selfsame sweet heat-rood
you fingered in solitude Denver or Brooklyn or fucked in a
    maiden in Paris carlots
please master drive me thy vehicle, body of love drops,
    sweat fuck
body of tenderness, Give me your dog fuck faster
please master make me go moan on the table
Go moan O please master do fuck me like that

in your rhythm thrill-plunge & pull-back-bounce & push
     down
till I loosen my asshole a dog on the table yelping with
     terror delight to be loved
Please master call me a dog, an ass beast, a wet asshole,
& fuck me more violent, my eyes hid with your palms
     round my skull
& plunge down in a brutal hard lash thru soft drip-fish
& throb thru five seconds to spurt out your semen heat
over & over, bamming it in while I cry out your name I do
     love you
please Master.

May 1968

A PROPHECY

O Future bards
chant from skull to heart to ass
as long as language lasts
Vocalize all chords
zap all consciousness
I sing out of mind jail
in New York State
without electricity
rain on the mountain
thought fills cities
I'll leave my body
in a thin motel
my self escapes
through unborn ears
Not my language
but a voice
chanting in patterns
survives on earth
not history's bones
but vocal tones
Dear breaths and eyes
shine in the skies
where rockets rise
to take me home

May 1968

BIXBY CANYON

Path crowded with thistle fern blue daisy,
     glassy grass, pale morninglory
         scattered on a granite hill
bells clanging under grey sea cliffs,
dry brackensprout seaweed-wreathed
where bee dies in sand hollows
         ant-swarmed above
white froth-wave glassed bay surge
     Ishvara-ripple on cave wall
           sea birds
     skating wind swell,
Amor Krishna Om Phat Svaha air rumble at
     ocean-lip
              Yesterday
Sand castles Neal, white plasm balls round
     jellies —
     Skeleton snaketubes & back
     nostrils' seaweed-tail dry-wrinkled
     brown seabulb & rednailed
     cactus blossom-petal tongues —
Brownpickle saltwater tomato ball
     rubber tail Spaghettied
        with leafmeat,
Mucous-softness crown'd Laurel thong-hat
     Father Whale gunk transparent
        yellowleaf egg-sac sandy
     lotos-petal cast back to cold
        watersurge.
           Bouquet of old seaweed
on a striped blanket, kelp tentacle spread
round the prayer place —

Hermes silver
firelight spread over wave sunglare —
The Cosmic Miasma Anxiety meditating nakedman
—Soft Bonepipe!
Musical Sea-knee gristlebone rubber
burp footswat beard ball bounce
of homosexual Shlurp ocean hish
Sabahadabadie Sound-limit
to Evil —
Set limit, set limit, set limit to
oceansong?
Limit birdcries, limit the Limitless
in language? O Say
Can You See The Internationale
Mental Traveller Marseillaise
in waves of eye alteration Politics?
'Tis sweet Liberty I hymn in freeman's sunlight
not limited to observe No Nakedness signs
in silent bud-crowded pathways, artforms
of flowers limitless Ignorance —
Wet seaweed blossoms froth left, sun breathing
giant mist under the bridge,
grey cliffs cloud-skin haloed
yellow sunlight of Old
shining on mossledge, tide foam
lapped in harmless gold light —
O Eyeball Brightness shimmering ! Father Circle
whence we have sprung, thru thy bright
Rainbow horn, Silence!
So sings the laborer under the rock bridge,
so pipes pray to the Avalanche.

June 16, 1968 / Big Sur, grass

CROSSING NATION

Under silver wing
    San Francisco's towers sprouting
         thru thin gas clouds,
   Tamalpais black-breasted above Pacific azure
      Berkeley hills pine-covered below —
Dr Leary in his brown house scribing Independence
                        Declaration
        typewriter at window
     silver panorama in natural eyeball —

Sacramento valley rivercourse's Chinese
      dragonflames licking green flats north-hazed
   State Capitol metallic rubble, dry checkered fields
     to Sierras—past Reno, Pyramid Lake's
     blue Altar, pure water in Nevada sands'
       brown wasteland scratched by tires

    Jerry Rubin arrested! Beaten, jailed,
            coccyx broken —
Leary out of action—"a public menace . . .
     persons of tender years . . . immature
         judgment . . . psychiatric examination . . ."
i.e. Shut up or Else   Loonybin or Slam

Leroi on bum gun rap, $7,000
      lawyer fees, years' negotiations —
SPOCK GUILTY headlined temporary, Joan Baez'
     paramour husband Dave Harris to Gaol
Dylan silent on politics, & safe —
     having a baby, a man —
Cleaver shot at, jail'd, maddened, parole revoked,

Vietnam War flesh-heap grows higher,
        blood splashing down the mountains of bodies
                on to Cholon's sidewalks —
Blond boys in airplane seats fed technicolor
        Murderers advance w/ Death-chords
            thru photo basement,
     Earplugs in, steak on plastic
              served—Eyes up to the Image —

What do I have to lose if America falls?
    my body? my neck? my personality?

June 19, 1968

Smoke Rolling Down Street

Red Scabies on the Skin
Police Cars turn Garbage Corner —
Was that a Shot! Backfire or Cherry Bomb?
Ah, it's all right, take the mouth off,
it's all over.

Man Came a long way,
Canoes thru Fire Engines,
Big Cities' power station Fumes
Executives with Country Houses —
Waters drip thru Ceilings in the Slum —
It's all right, take the mouth off
it's all over —

June 23, 1968, N.Y.

PERTUSSIN

Always Ether Comes
    to dissuade the
        goat-like
            sensible —
or N_2O recurring to
    elicit ironic
        suicidal pen marks —
Parallels: in Montmartre   Rousseau
    daubing or Rimbaud arriving,
        the raw Aether
shines with Brahmanic cool moonshine
    aftertaste, midnight Nostalgia.

June 28, 1968

Swirls of Black Dust on Avenue D

white haze over Manhattan's towers
    midsummer green Cattail's fatness
      surrounding Hoboken Marsh
             garbage Dumps,

Wind over Pulaski Skyway's
    lacy networks
Trucks crash Bayonne's roadways,
    iron engines roar

Stink rises over Hydro Pruf Factory
Cranes lift over broken earth
Brain Clouds boil out tin-cone scrap burners
        Newark sits in grey gas
        July heat gleams on airplanes
Trailer tyres sing toward forests of oiltowers,
Power grids dance in th' Iron Triangle,
      Tanks roast in Flatness —
Old Soybean-oil-storage Scandals
            echo thru airwaves,
the family car bumps over asphalt toward Bright Mexico.

July 10, 1968

VIOLENCE

Mexcity drugstore table, giant
    sexfiend in black spats
Sticks knife in a plump faggot's
    sportscoat seam;
at Teotihuacan in blue sunlight, I slap
    my mocking blond nephew
    for getting lost on the Moon
    Pyramid.
In Oakland, legendary police shoot a
    naked black boy running out
    of his political basement
In Pentagon giant machines humm and
    bleep in neon arcades,
Buttons click in sockets & robots
    pencil prescriptions for acid gas
    sunsets —
New York on the stairway, the dumbed
    whitefaced Junkey pulls a knife
    and stares immobile—the victim
    gasps, "oh come off it" & a sixpack
    of cokebottles
bounces down worn black steps, in
    Vietnam plastic fire
Streams down myriad phantom cheeks
    rayed over planet television —
Adrenalin runs in armpits from Los Angeles
    to Paris, Harlem & Cannes
explode thru plateglass, Sunset Strip & Sorbonne
    are crowded with Longhaired angels
    armed with gasmasks & Acid,
& Angry Democrats gather in Chicago

 fantasizing armies running
  thru Sewers sprayed with Mace.
I walk up Avenida Juarez, over
  cobbled shadows, blue-tiled streetlamps
lighting Sanborns' arcades, behind me violent
  chic fairy gangsters with bloody hands
hustle after midnight to cut my throat from
  its beard.

July 22, 1968
4:30 AM

PAST SILVER DURANGO OVER
MEXIC SIERRA WRINKLES

Westward Mother-mountains drift Pacific, green-sloped
    canyons vaster than Mexico City
without roads under cloud-flowers bearing tiny shadow-
    blossoms on vegetable peaks —
red riverbeds snake thru paradises without electricity
— Huichol or Tarahumara solitudes hectare'd irregular,
    antpaths to rocky plateaux,
hollows for lone indian humility, hand-ploughed moun-
    tainside patches —
naked white cloud-fronds floating silent over silent green
    earth-crags.
O vast meccas of manlessness, Bright cloud-brains tower'd
    in blue space up to the Sun
with rainbow garlands over white water-gas, O tree-furred
    body defenseless thru clear air, visible green breast
    of America!
vaster than man the Mother Mountains manifest nakedness
    greater than all the bombs Bacteria ever invented
Impregnable cloud-cities adrift & dissolving no History,
white rain-ships alighted in Zenith Blue Ocean —
No ports or capitals to the horizon, emerald mesas ridged
    infinite-budded
where rivers and ants gather garbage man left behind in the
    Valley of Mexico —
Iron'll rust under living tree roots & soak back under-
    ground
to feed the sensitive tendrils of Ego covering mountains of
    granite green mossed unconscious.
Heaven & ocean mirror their azure, horizon lost in yel-
    lowed spectrum-mist —

Baja California Blue water lies flat to the brown armpit of
     United States,
River's course muddies the delta with teardrops washed
     dusty from Utah — Green irrigated farm squares in
     desert —
& the dung colored gas, brown haze of labor near Los
     Angeles risen the height of Sierras —
grey smog drifts thru low mountain passes, city invisible.
                    Floating armchairs descend
from sky in sunlight, rocking back & forth in polluted
     fields of air.

July 22, 1968
11AM

ON NEAL'S ASHES

Delicate eyes that blinked blue Rockies all ash
nipples, Ribs I touched w/ my thumb are ash
mouth my tongue touched once or twice all ash
bony cheeks soft on my belly are cinder, ash
earlobes & eyelids, youthful cock tip, curly pubis
breast warmth, man palm, high school thigh,
baseball bicept arm, asshole anneal'd to silken skin
all ashes, all ashes again.

August 1968

GOING TO CHICAGO

22,000 feet over Hazed square Vegetable planet Floor
Approaching Chicago to Die or flying over Earth another
    40 years
to die—Indifferent, and Afraid, that the bone-shattering
    bullet
be the same as the vast evaporation-of-phenomena Cancer
Come true in an old man's bed. Or Historic
Fire-Heaven Descending 22,000 years End th' Atomic
    Aeon

The Lake's blue again, Sky's the same baby, tho' papers &
    Noses
rumor tar spread through the Natural Universe'll make
    Angel's feet sticky.
I heard the Angel King's voice, a bodiless tuneful teenager
Eternal in my own heart saying "Trust the Purest Joy —
Democratic Anger is an Illusion, Democratic Joy is God
Our Father is baby blue, the original face you see Sees
    You —"

How, thru Conventional Police & Revolutionary Fury
Remember the Helpless order the Police Armed to protect,
The Helpless Freedom the Revolutionary Conspired to
    honor —
I am the Angel King sang the Angel King
as mobs in Amphitheaters, Streets, Colosseums Parks and
    offices
Scream in despair over Meat and Metal Microphone

Aug. 24, 1968

GRANT PARK: AUGUST 28, 1968

Green air, children sat under trees with the old,
bodies bare, eyes open to eyes under the hotel wall,
the ring of Brown-clothed bodies armed
     but silent at ease leaned on their rifles —

Harsh sound of mikrophones, helicopter roar —
A current in the belly, future marches
     and detectives naked in bed —
where? on the planet, not Chicago,
     in late sunlight —

Miserable picnic, Police State or Garden of Eden?
in the building walled against the sky
magicians exchange images, Money vote
     and handshakes —
The teargas drifted up to the Vice
     President naked in the bathroom
—naked on the toilet taking a shit weeping?
Who wants to be President of the
     Garden of Eden?

CAR CRASH

I

Snow-blizzard sowing
ice-powder drifts on stone fenced
gardens near grey woods.

Yellow hump-backed snow plough
rocking giant tires round
the road, red light flashing
iron insect brain.

Mrow, the cat with diarrhea.

Sunlight settled into human form,
tree rings settled age after age
stone forests accumulating atoms
travelled 93,000,000 miles,
carbon deposits settled into beds,
the mountain's head breathes light,
Earth-hairs gather gold beams
thru chlorophyl, poets walk
between the green bushes
sprouting solar language.

Broken bones in bed,
hips and ribs cracked by autos,
snowdrifts over rubber tires,
tree stumps freeze, the body stump
heals temporarily in wintertime.

II

So that's it the body, ah!
Beat yr meat in a dark bed.
Boy friends wrinkle & shit in snow.
Girls go fat-eyed to their mother's coffin.

Cigarettes burned my tastebuds' youth,
I smelled my lover's behind,
This autocrash broke my hip and ribs,
Ugh, Thud, nausea-breath at solar plexus
paralysed my bowels four days —
Eyeglasses broke, eyeballs still intact —
Thank God! alas, still alive but talk words
died in my body, thoughts died in pain.

A healthy day in the snow, white breath
and warm wool sox, hat over ears, hot broth,
nakedness in warm boudoirs, stiff prick come,
fame, physic, learning, scepter, dusk
and Aurora Borealis, hot pig flesh, turkey
stuffing—all disappear in a broken skull.

Unstable element, Sight Sound flesh Touch
& Taste, all Odour, one more consciousness
backseat of a steaming auto with broken nose —
Unstable place to be, an easy way out
by metal crash instead of mind cancer.
Unreliable meat, waving a chicken bone
in a hospital bed—get what's coming to you
like the chicken steak you ate last year.
Impossible Dr. Feelgood Forever, gotta die
made of worm-stuff. And worm thoughts?

And who's left watching, or even

remembers the car crash that severed
the skull from the spinal column?
Who gets out of body, or who's shut in
a box of soft pain when Napalm drops
from Heaven all over the abdomen,
breasts and cheek-skin? & tongue cut out
by inhuman knives? Cow tongue? Man tongue?

What does it feel like not to talk?
To die in the back seat, Ow!

21 Dec 68

III

Raw pine walls, ice-white windows
three weeks now, snowy flatness
foot-thick down valley meadows,
wind roar in bare ash arms, oak branch
tendrils icy gleaming, yellow
stain of morning water in front
door's snow—I walk out on crutches
to see white moonglow make snow blue
—three men just rode a space ship
round the moon last week—gnashing
their teeth in Biafra & Palestine,
Assassins & Astronauts travelling from
Athens to the sea of Venus Creatrix —
Lover's quarrels magnified decades to mad
violence, half naked farm boys stand
with axes at the kitchen table,
trembling guilty, slicing egg
grapefruit breasts on breakfast oilcloth.
Growing old, growing old, forget the words,
mind jumps to the grave, forget words,

Love's an old word, forget words,
Peter with shave-head beardface
mutters & screams to himself at midnight.
A new year, no party tonite, forget
old loves, old words, old feelings.
Snow everywhere around the house,
I turned off the gas-light & came upstairs
alone to read, remembering pictures of dead
moon-side, my hip broken, the cat sick,
earhead filled with my own strong music,
in a houseful of men, sleep in underwear.
Neal almost a year turned to ash, angel
in his own midnight without a phonecall,
Jack drunk in my mind or his Florida.
Forget old friends, old words, old loves,
old bodies. Bhaktivedanta advises Christ.
The body lies in bed in '69 alone,
a gnostic book fills the lap, Aeons
revolve 'round the household, Rimbaud
age 16 adolescent sneers tight lipt
green-eyed oval in old time gravure
—1869 his velvet tie askew, hair
mussed & ruffled by policeman's rape.

1:30 AM Jan 1, 1969

IV

Ecologues of These States

1969-1971

OVER DENVER AGAIN

Grey clouds blot sunglare, mountains float west, plane
softly roaring over Denver—Neal dead a year—clean suburb
     yards,
fit boardinghouse for the homosexual messenger's
alleyway Lila a decade back before the Atombomb.
Denver without Neal, eh? Denver with orange sunsets
& giant airplanes winging silvery to San Francisco —
watchtowers thru red cold planet light, when the Earth
     Angel's dead
the dead material planet'll revolve robotlike
& insects hop back and forth between metallic cities.

Feb 13, 1969

Rising over Night-blackened Detroit Streets

brilliant network-lights tentacle dim suburbs
Michigan waters canalled glittering thru city building
    blocks
Throne-brain lamps strung downtown, green signals'
concentrate brightness blinking metal prayers & bright
    Hare Krishnas
telepathic to Heavenly darkness whence I stare down and
    adore O beautiful!
Mankind maker of such contemplate machine! Come
    gentle brainwaves
delicate-soft heart-throbs tender as belly butterflies,
light as Sexual charm-penumbras be, of radiant-eyed
boys & girls black-faced & blond that Born believe
Earth-death at hand, or Eden regenerate millennial Green
their destiny under your Human Police Will, O
Masters, fathers, mayors, Senators, Presidents, Bankers &
    workers
sweating & weeping ignorant on your own plastic-pain
    Maya planet . . .

February 15, 1969

IMAGINARY UNIVERSES

Under orders to shoot the spy, I discharged
    my pistol into his mouth.
He fell face down from the position life
    left his body kneeling blindfold.

No, I never did that. Imagined in airport snow,
    Albany plane discharging passengers.

Yes, the Mexican-faced boy, 19
    in Marine cloth, seat next me
Descending Salt Lake, accompanied his
    brother's body from Vietnam.
"The Gook was kneeling in front of me,
    crying & pleading. There were two;
    He had a card we dropped on them."
The card granted immunity to those
    V.C. surrendering.
"On account of my best friend &
    my brother I killed both Gooks."
That was true, yes.

February 1969

TO POE: OVER THE PLANET,
AIR ALBANY-BALTIMORE

Albany   throned in snow
          Hudson ribboned North ice white flats
New England's blue sky horizon'd to Space
          Age eyes: Man rides the Map,
Earth ballooned vast-bottomed . . .

It's winter, Poe, upstate New York scythed
          into mental fields, flat arbors & hairy woods
          scattered in Pubic mounds twittering w/ birds —
Nobody foresaw these wormpaths asphalted
          uphill crost bridges to small church towns, chill
          snowfields streaked with metal feces-dust.
Maelstrom roar of air-boats to Baltimore!
Farmland whirlpooled into mechanic apocalypse
          on Iron Tides!
 . . . . .Wheels drop in Sunlight, over
          Vast building-hive roofs glittering,
New York's ice agleam
          in a dying world.
                    Bump down to ground
Hare Krishna Preserver!

Philadelphia smoking in Gold Sunlight, pink blue
          green Cyanide tanks sitting on hell's floor,
Many chimneys smoldering, city flats virus-linked
          along Delaware bays under horizon-smog —
airplane drifting black vapor-filaments
          above Wilmington — — The iron habitations
          endless from Manhattan to the Capital.
Poe! D'jya prophesy this Smogland, this Inferno,

Didja Dream Baltimore'd Be Seen From Heaven
by Man Poet's eyes Astounded in the Fire Haze,
                              carbon Gas aghast!
Poe! D'jya know yr prophecies' RED DEATH
would pour thru Philly's sky like Sulfurous Dreams?
Walled into Amontillado's Basement! Man
        kind led weeping drunk into the Bomb
        Shelter by Mad Secretaries of Defense!

South! from the Bearded Sleeper's Wink
at History, Hudson polluted & Susquehanna
        Brown under bridges laced with factory smoke —
Proving grounds by Chesapeake,
                    Ammunition & Artillery
Edgewood & Aberdeen
                    Chemical munitions factories
hid isolate in wooden gardens, Princesses
of Industry (like Movie stars hid private in Magic
        Nauseous Mansions in Old Hollywood) —
Poe! Frankenstein! Shelley thy Prophecy,
What Demiurge assembles Matter-Factories
        to blast the Cacodemonic Planet-Mirror apart
Split atoms & Polarize Consciousness &
        let the eternal Void leak thru Pentagon
& cover White House with Eternal Vacuum-Dust!
Bethlehem's miles of Christ-birth Man-apocalypse
        Mechano-movie Refinery along Atlantic,
Shit-brown haze worse & worse over Baltimore
        where Poe's world came to end—Red smoke,
Black water, grey sulphur clouds over Sparrows Point
        Oceanside flowing with rust, scum tide
        boiling shoreward —

Red white blue yachts on Baltimore harbor,
        the plane bounds down above gas tanks,

gas stations, smokestacks flaring poison mist,
Superhighways razored thru hairy woods,
Down to Earth Man City where Poe
     Died kidnapped by phantoms
conspiring to win elections
     in the Deathly Gutter of 19th Century.

March 1969

EASTER SUNDAY

Slope woods' snows melt
Streams gush, ducks stand one foot
beak eye buried in backfeathers,
Jerusalem pillars' gold sunlight
yellow in window-shine, bright
rays spikey-white flashed in mud,
coo coo ripples thru maple branch,
horse limps head down, pale grass shoots
green winter's brown vegetable
hair—washed by transparent trickling
ice water freshets
earth's rusty slough bathed clean,
streams ripple leaf-bottomed
channels sounded vocal, white light
afternoon sky end —

Goat bells move, black kids bounce,
butting mother's hairy side & tender tit
one maa'ing child hangs under Bessie's udder
ducks waggle yellow beaks, new grass flooded,
Tiger cat maeows on barn straw,
herb patch by stone wall's a shiny marsh,
dimpling snow water glimmers, birds whistle
from icecrystal beds under bare bushes,
breeze blows rooster crow thru chill light
extended from the piney horizon.

1969

FALLING ASLEEP IN AMERICA

We're in the Great Place, Fable Place, Beulah, Man wedded
    to Earth, Planet of green Grass
Tiny atomic wheels spin shining, worlds change Heavens
    inside out, the planet's reborn in ashes,
Sun lights sparkle on atomic cinder, plants levitate, green
    moss precedes trees trembling sentient,
Stone eats blue skies solar dazzle with invisible mouths &
    flowers are the rocks' excrement —

Each million years atoms spin myriad reversals, worlds in
    worlds interchange populations —
from worm to man's a tiny jump from earth to earth souls
    are borne ever forgetful —
populations eat their own meat, roses smell sweet in the
    faeces of horses risen red-fac'd.
Consciousness changes nightly, dreams flower new uni-
    verses in brainy skulls.

Lying in bed body darkened ear of the bus roar running,
    only the eye flickering grass green returns me to
    Nashville.

April 1969

NORTHWEST PASSAGE

Incense under Horse Heaven Hills
Empty logger trucks speed
            Lake Wallula's flatness shimmering
Under Hat Rock painted w/
                white highschool signs.
Chemical smoke boils up
        under aluminum-bright cloud-roof —
Smog assembling over railroad
        cars parked rusting on thin rails —
Factory looming vaster than Johnson
            Butte—Look at that Shit!
Smell it! Got about 30 smokestacks going!
Polluting Wallula! Boise Cascade —
            Container Corp!
The Package is the Product, onomatopoeticized
                McLuhan in '67 —
Wall Street Journal Apr. 22 full
        page ad Proclaimed:

We got the trees! We got
        the land beneath!
We Gotta invent More Forms
        for Cardboard Country!
We'll dig forests for Genius
        Spirit God Stuff Gold-root
for Sale on Wall Street. Give
        us your money! order
        our cardboard Wastebaskets!
We just invented throwaway Planets!

Trees crash in Heaven! Sulphurous Urine

pours thru Boise, Chevron & Brea
      Wastepipes where Snake & Wallula
           ripple shining
Where Sakajawea led White Men thru blue sky
         fresh sweet water roads
      Towards mountains of juicy
         telepathic pine & open Thalassa
      Thalassa! Green salt waves
           washing rock mountains, Pacific

Sirhan lives!
      to hear his jury say
"We now fix the penalty at Death."

Green salt waves washing Wall Street.
Rain on grey sage near Standard
      Oil junction Eltopia,
Static at Mesa! Yodelling ancient
      Prajnaparamita
Gaté Gaté Paragaté Parasamgaté
         Bodhi Svaha!
Way Down Yonder in the Bayoux
      Country in Dear old Louisian,
Hank Williams chanting to country
         Nature, electric
wires run up rolling brownploughed wheatfields —
Wallula polluted! Wallula polluted! Wallula polluted!

"For most large scale gambling enterprises to continue over any extended period of time, the cooperation of corrupt Police or local officials is necessary." P. 1 *Oregonian,* "Mapping a $61 million war against organized crime, President Nixon suggested . . ."

"Even Jesus Christ couldn't have
saved me." Sirhan . . .
                "shed no tears.
                        His face was ashen"
                                        A.P.
                America's heart Broken,

Chessman, Vietnam, Sirhan.
52% People thought the War
                always had been a mistake,
                        by April 1969.

May Day parade cancelled for Prague
                says Police Radio to
                        the old King of May faraway —
SDS chanting thru consciousness megaphones
                in every university.
By now, Beatles & Beach Boys have
                entered the Sublime
thru Acid The Crist of Kali Yuga, thru
                Transcendental Meditation,
Chanting Hare Krishna climbing Eiffel Tower,
Apollinaire & Mira Bai headless
                together with Kabir transmitted
over Apocalyptic Radios, their voice-
                vibrations roaring
thru a million loudspeakers in Green
                Autos on the world's roads —
Matter become so thick, senses so sunk
                in Chickens & Insulation
"Love aint gonna die, I'm gonna haveta
                kill it"
god cries to himself, Christ merging with
                Krishna in Car Crash Salvation!

"Prosecutor John Howard called Sirhan a cold-blooded
political assassin with *'no special claim to further preserva-
tion.'* "

Mao reelected Chinese Premier.

Where the Mullan Rd
     meets route 26
          by 2 giant Sycamores
     approaching Hooper,
Has anyone here any "Special
          claim to further preservation"?

These lambs grazing thru springtime
               by Cow Creek, quiet in
     American yellow light —
"Even J.C. couldn't have saved me."

Magpie, Meadowlark, rainbow
       apparitions shafted transparent
    down from grey cloud.
                 Dogs see
                 in black & white.

A complete half-rainbow
     hill to hill across the highway
pots of gold anchoring the pretty bridge,
          tumbleweed passing underneath

"Saigon (AP) U.S. B52 bombers made their heaviest raids
of the Vietnam War last night near the Cambodian border,
dropping more than 2,000 tons of bombs along a 30 mile
stretch Northwest of Saigon, the US COMMAND reported.
'They are harassing enemy troops so as not to let them get
organized,' an American SPOKESMAN said."

Czech student strikes unreported in Prague

Howard Marquette & George Washington U. sit-in:
Hail on new-ploughed brown hilltops —
Black rainclouds and rainbows over Albion way —
Drive down valley to Main Street
       Seattle First National Motor
    next to Everybody's Bank.

April 24, 1969

SONORA DESERT-EDGE

Om Ah Hūṃ Vajra Guru
Padma Siddhi Hūṃ
—Drum H. from Gary S.
from Tarthang Tulku

Brown stonepeaks   rockstumps
                    cloudless sunlight
Saguaro green arms praying up
        spine ribs risen
                    woodpecker-holed
        nose-pricked limbs
            lifted salutation —
orange flower eyes lifted on
        needley Ocotillo stalk
Jumping Cholla pistils closing pollened
        eyebrow-vagina buds to the
            poked pinkey —
Palo Verde smooth forked branch
            above prickly-pear ears

Smoke plumed up white
        from scratched desert plain,
        chemical smoke, military copper
            airplanes rotting,
                    4% Copper Smelter smog

—in wire cage, ivory hook-beaked
                    round black pupiled
        Bald Eagle's head, tailfeathers
        hung below claw'd branch, symmetric

body plumes brown webbed like dollarbills,
     insecticides sterilized many
          adults

—green duck neck sheen spectral as
       moon machines
Raven hopping curious black beaked
Coyote's nose sensitive lifted to air
        blinking eye sharp
as the rose bellied Cardinal's ivory whistle

—tiny bright statues of Buddha
     standing,
     blue desert valley haze —
     cactus lessons in sentience,
Trees like metal carrots — Anaconda
     smelters   white plumesmoke in
     San Manuel, or Phelps-Dodge
     in Douglas? —
Yellow'd Creosote bushes in granular
     dust, hills jeep tracked,
Prairie dogs stand quivering-spined in
     cactus-shade.   A museum,
     minds in Ashramic City—tweetling
     bird radios—Hopi Rain:

April 29, 1969

REFLECTIONS IN SLEEPY EYE

For Robert Bly

3,489 friendly people
Elm grove, willow, Blue Earth County's
    red barns, tiny feoff with
    gas nozzle snout on hillock,
Large beetles & lizards —
        orange-painted steel
        cranes & truck cabs,
    Green seeder down-pointed
          Science Toy earth-cock.
Thin floods, smooth planted acres
        upturned, brown
    cornstubble ploughed under,
    tractor pulling discs over fenced land.
Old box-alder fallen over
    on knees in pond-flood,
white painted gas tanks by
    Springfield's rail yard woods,
        tiny train parade by Meats
        Groceries North Star Seeds
Our Flag at full mast
    TV antennae, large leafy antennaed
        trees upstretched green,
        trunks standing sunlit
    Sheep on stormfenced knoll,
        green little wood acres —
    one forest from Canada to these
    plains—Corn silage in net bins,

Windmills in Tracy,
Blue enamel silos cap'd
aluminum, minarets in white sunbeam.
Cannabis excellent for drying lymph-
glands, specific relief for
symptoms of colds, flu,
ear pressure grippe &
Eustachean tube clogging —
A tree, bent broken mid-trunk
branches to ground —
Much land, few folk, excelsior grave
yard stones
silver tipp'd phalloi to heaven —
Aum, Om, Ford, Mailbox
telephone pole wire strung
down road. Lake house
fence poles, tree shade
pine hill grave, Ah
Lake Benton's blue waved waters —
finally, Time came to
the brick barn! collapsed!
Old oak trunk sunk thick
under ground.
Farm car ploughman rolling discs,
iron cuts smooth ground even,
hill plains roll —
Cows browse under alder shoot,
bent limbs arch clear brown
stream beds, trees stand
on banks observing
shade, peculiar standing up or kneeling
groundward
Car graveyard fills eyes
iron glitters, chrome fenders

      rust —
White crosses, Vietnam War Dead
           churchbells ring
Cars, kids, hamburger stand
      open, barn-smile
         white eye, door mouth.

May 9, 1969

INDEPENDENCE DAY

Orange hawkeye stronger than thought winking above a
    thousand thin grassblades —
Dr. Hermon busted in Texas for green weed garden-grown
licensed Federal, Municipal-cop-prosecuted nathless —
Sweet chirrup from bush top to bush top, orange wing'd
birds' scratch-beaked telegraphy signalled to and fro but-
    tercup earlets —
warbles & sweet whistles swifting echo-noted by fly buzz,
jet-roar rolling down thru clouds —
So tiny a grasshopper climbing timothy stub the birds
    can't tell they're there —
intense soft leaf-spears budding symmetric,
breeze bending gentle flowerheads against yarrow their
    persons —
eyelids heavy, summer heavy with fear, mapletrunks heavy
    with green leaf-mass —
closed buds of hawkeye stronger than thought tremble on
    tall hairy stems.

      .   .   .   .   .   .

Red shelled bedbugs crawl war sheets,
city garbage spoils wet sidewalks where children play —
A telephone call from Texas tells the latest police-state
    bust.
O Self tangled in TV wires, white judges and laws
your jet-thunder echoes in clouds, your DDT spread thru
    firmament waters poisons algae & brown pelican —
Smog veils Maya, paranoia walks great cities in blue suits
    with guns,
— are all these billion grassblades safe?
My stomach's bitter, city haste & money loss, —
Hawkeye stronger than thought! Horsefly and bee!

St. John's wort nodding yellow bells at the sun! eyes
        close in your presence, I
lie in your soft green bed, watch light thru red lid-skin,
        language persistent as birdwarble in my brain.
Independence Day! the Cow's deep moo's an Aum!

1969

I WANT! I WANT!

IN A MOONLIT HERMIT'S CABIN

Watching the White Image, electric moon, white mist drift-
ing over woods
St. John's Wort & Hawkeye wet with chance Yarrow on
the green hillside
"D'ya want your Airline Transport Pilot to smoke grass?
Want yr moon-men to smoke loco weed?"
What Comedy's this Epic! The lamb lands on the Alcohol
Sea—Deep voices
"A Good batch of Data"—The hours of Man's first landing
on the moon —
One and a Half Million starv'd in Biafra—Football players
broadcast cornflakes —
TV mentioned America as much as Man—Brillo offers you
free Moon-Map— 2 labels —
And CBS repeats Man-Epic—Now here again is Walter
Cronkite,
"How easy these words . . . a shiver down the old spine . . .
Russia soundly beaten! China one Fifth of Mankind, no
word broadcast . . ."
The Queen watched the moon-landing at Windsor Castle —
Pulling a fast one on Hypnosis at Disneyland, the Ker-
chief-headed Crowd
Waving to the TV Camera—Ersatz Moon —
"No place gives you history today except the Moon" —
Running behind time entering Space Suits —
And a Moon-in at Central Sheep Meadow —
Western Electric's solemn moment!

And rain in the woods drums on the old cabin!
I want! I want! a ladder from the depths of the forest
night to the silvery moon-wink —
A flag on the reporter's space-suit shoulder —

Peter Groaning & Cursing in bed, relieved of the lunatic
    burden at last —

'Tis Tranquillity base where the Tragedy will settle the
    Eve.
Alert for solar flares, clock ticks, static from Antennae —
    swift as death.
I didn't think we'd see this Night.
Plant the flag and you're doomed! Life a dream—slumber
    in eyes of woods,
Antennae scraping the ceiling. Static & Rain!
Saw the earth in Dream age 37, half cloud-wrapped, from a
    balcony in outer-space —
Méliès—giddiness—picture tube gaga —
"Men land on Sun!" decennial sentences —
Announcers going goofy muttering "142—"
Alone in space: Dump Pressure in the LEM!
Hare Krishna! Lift m' Dorje on the kitchen table!
No Science Fiction expected this Globe-Eye Consciousness
Simultaneous with opening a hatch on Heaven.
A moth in the Déjà Vu!
This is the instant—open the hatch—every second is dust in
    the hourglass—Hatch open!
The Virus will grow green slime reptiles in sixty centuries,
& gobble up their fathers as we ate up God —
Imagine dying Tonight! Closing the eyes on the man in the
    Moon!
Sighing away forever ... everyone got sleepy ... On the
    moon porch —

A 38 year old human American standing on the surface of
    the moon —
Footprint on the Charcoal dust — stepped out
and it's the old familiar Moon, as undersea or mountain-
    top, a place —
"Very pretty on the Moon!" oh, 'twere Solid Gold —

Voices calling "Houston to Moon" — Two "Americans" on
    the moon!
Beautiful view, bouncing the surface—"one quarter of the
    world denied these pix by their rulers"!
Setting up the flag!

July Moon Day '69

Rain-wet asphalt heat, garbage curbed cans overflowing

I hauled down lifeless mattresses to sidewalk refuse-piles,
old rugs stept on from Paterson to Lower East Side filled
    with bed-bugs,
grey pillows, couch seats treasured from the street laid
    back on the street
—out, to hear Murder-tale, 3rd Street cyclists attacked to-
    nite —
Bopping along in rain, Chaos fallen over City roofs,
shrouds of chemical vapour drifting over building-tops —
Get the *Times,* Nixon says peace reflected from the Moon,
but I found no boy body to sleep with all night on pave-
    ments 3 AM home in sweating drizzle —
Those mattresses soggy lying by full five garbagepails —
Barbara, Maretta, Peter Steven Rosebud slept on these Pil-
    lows years ago,
forgotten names, also made love to me, I had these mat-
    tresses four years on my floor —
Gerard, Jimmy many months, even blond Gordon later,
Paul with the beautiful big cock, that teenage boy that
    lived in Pennsylvania,
forgotten numbers, young dream loves and lovers, earthly
    bellies —
many strong youths with eyes closed, come sighing and
    helping me come —
Desires already forgotten, tender persons used and kissed
    goodbye
and all the times I came to myself alone in the dark dream-
    ing of Neal or Billy Budd
—nameless angels of half-life—heart beating & eyes weeping
    for lovely phantoms —
Back from the Gem Spa, into the hallway, a glance behind
and sudden farewell to the bedbug-ridden mattresses piled
    soggy in dark rain.

August 2, 1969

DEATH ON ALL FRONTS

"The Planet is Finished"

A new moon looks down on our sick sweet planet
Orion's chased the Immovable Bear halfway across the sky
from winter to winter. I wake, earlier in bed, fly corpses
cover gas lit sheets, my head aches, left temple
brain fibre throbbing for Death I Created on all Fronts.
Poisoned rats in the Chickenhouse and myriad lice
Sprayed with white arsenics filtering to the brook, City
       Cockroaches
stomped on Country kitchen floors. No babies for me.
Cut earth boys & girl hordes by half & breathe free
say Revolutionary expert Computers:
Half the blue globe's germ population's more than enough,
keep the cloudy lung from stinking pneumonia.
I called in Exterminator Who soaked the Wall floor with
bed-bug death-oil. Who'll soak my brain with death-oil?
I wake before dawn, dreading my wooden possessions,
my gnostic books, my loud mouth, old loves silent, charms
turned to image money, my body sexless fat, Father dying,
Earth Cities poisoned at war, my art hopeless —
Mind fragmented—and still abstract—Pain in
left temple living death —

Sept. 26, 1969

MEMORY GARDENS

          covered with yellow leaves
              in morning rain

—Quel Deluge
          he threw up his hands
              & wrote the Universe dont exist
              & died to prove it.

Full Moon over Ozone Park
          Airport Bus rushing thru dusk to
                      Manhattan,
Jack the Wizard in his
                  grave at Lowell
for the first nite —
That Jack thru whose eyes I
          saw
       smog glory light
          gold over Mannahatta's spires
       will never see these
          chimneys smoking
anymore over statues of Mary
          in the graveyard

Black misted canyons
              rising over the bleak
                      river
Bright doll-like ads
          for Esso Bread —
Replicas multiplying beards
          Farewell to the Cross —
Eternal fixity, the big headed
          wax painted Buddha doll
              pale resting incoffined —

Empty-skulled New
        York streets
Starveling phantoms
     filling city —
Wax dolls walking park
         Ave,
Light gleam in eye glass
Voice echoing thru Microphones
Grand Central Sailor's
       arrival 2 decades later
          feeling melancholy —
Nostalgia for Innocent World
     War II —
A million corpses running
     across 42'd street
Glass buildings rising higher
          transparent
            aluminum —
artificial trees, robot sofas,
     Ignorant cars —
One Way Street to Heaven.

. . . .

Grey Subway Roar

A wrinkled brown faced fellow
         with swollen hands
leans to the blinking plate glass
     mirroring white poles, the heavy car
     sways on tracks uptown to Columbia —
Jack no more'll step off at Penn Station
     anonymous erranded, eat sandwich
     & drink beer near New Yorker Hotel or walk
under the shadow of Empire State.
Didn't we stare at each other length of the car
     & read headlines in faces thru Newspaper Holes?

Sexual cocked & horny bodied young, look
      at beauteous Rimbaud & Sweet Jenny
         riding to class from Columbus Circle.
"Here the kindly dopefiend lived."

and the rednecked sheriff beat the longhaired
         boy on the ass.
—103'd street Broadway, me & Hal abused for sidewalk
           begging twenty-five years ago.
Can I go back in time & lay my head on a teenage
         belly upstairs on 110'th Street?
or step off the iron car with Jack
        at the blue-tiled Columbia sign?
at last the old brown station where I had
a holy vision's been rebuilt, clean ceramic
over the scum & spit & come of quarter century.

———————————————

Flying to Maine in a trail of black smoke
Kerouac's obituary conserves *Time's*
         Front Paragraphs —
Empire State in Heaven Sun Set Red,
        White mist in old October
         over the billion trees of Bronx —
           There's too much to see —
Jack saw sun set red over Hudson horizon
        Two three decades back
thirtynine fourtynine fiftynine
          sixtynine
John Holmes pursed his lips,
         wept tears.
Smoke plumed up from oceanside chimneys
        plane roars toward Montauk
         stretched in red sunset —

Northport, in the trees, Jack drank
        rot gut & made haikus of birds
                tweetling on his porch rail at dawn —
Fell down and saw Death's golden lite
        in Florida garden a decade ago.
Now taken utterly, soul upward,
        & body down in wood coffin
            & concrete slab-box.
I threw a kissed handful of damp earth
        down on the stone lid
                & sighed
        looking in Creeley's one eye,
Peter sweet holding a flower
        Gregory toothless bending his
                knuckle to Cinema machine —
and that's the end of the drabble tongued
        Poet who sounded his Kock-rup
                throughout the Northwest Passage.
Blue dusk over Saybrook, Holmes
                sits down to dine Victorian —
& *Time* has a ten-page spread on
        Homosexual Fairies!

Well, while I'm here I'll
        do the work —
and what's the Work?
        To ease the pain of living.
Everything else, drunken
                dumbshow.

                                    October 22-29, 1969

FLASH BACK

In a car Grey smoke over Elmira
The vast boy reformatory brick factory
Valed below misty hills 25 years ago
I sat with Joe Army visiting and murmured green Grass.
Jack's just not *here* anymore, Neal's ashes
Loneliness makes old men moan, God's solitude,
O women shut up, yelling for baby meat more.

Nov 10, 1969

GRAFFITI 12TH CUBICLE MEN'S ROOM
SYRACUSE AIRPORT

11 November 1969

I am married and would like to fuck someone else
Have a strange piece (Go Home)
USN '69
I want to suck a big cock Make Date
Support Third World Struggle Against US Imperialism
I fucked Mom and got VD
All power to the Viet Cong!
Yeah! Max Voltage up the Ass!! Ω
Perhaps Man needs—But to kill is only brown butter Wax
April 20, 1965   Mike Heck & Salena Bennett
Keep on Chugglin
Eat prunes and be a regular guy.
I would like to suck a big cock.
So would I.
War is good business Invest your son.
Help me J.P.
John Wayne flunked basic training.
Pat Miller '69 Home on Leave
My wife sucks cock.
Chickenman Lives Yes somewhere in Argentina
Peace & Love Sucks
I want a blow job Who do I call
What if someone gave a war & Nobody came?
Life would ring the bells of Ecstasy and Forever be Itself
        again.
J. Edgar Hoover F.B.I. is a Voyeur.
Man, I'm really stoned out of my skull really O-Zoned—
        good old LSD the colors in here are so nice really
        fine colors and the floor tile is really outasight if

you haven't tried it you ought to since it is the only way to really get your head together by first getting it apart LSD Forever.

$CH2CH2N(CH3)2$

AFTER THOUGHTS

When he kissed my nipple
    I felt elbow bone thrill —
When lips touched my belly
    tickle ran up to my ear
When he took my cock head to tongue
      a tremor shrunk sphincter, joy
          shuddered my reins
I breathed deep sighing ahh!

—   —   —   —   —   —

Mirror looking, combing
    grey glistening beard
Were I found sharp eyed
    attractive to the young?
Bad magic or something —
Foolish magic most likely.

November 1969

G. S. READING POESY AT PRINCETON

Gold beard combd down like chinese fire   gold hair braid-
    ed at skull-nape—
gold turning silver soon—worn face young forehead wrin-
    kled, deep-boned smile,
tiny azure earring, turquoise finger stone, Paramita beads
    centered by ivory skull-nut —
On Deer Mountain, in ship's iron belly, sat crosslegged on
    Princeton couch,
body voice rumbling Bear Sutra to younger selves—her
    long hair to rug, dungareed legs lotus-postured;
or that half-Indian boy his face so serious woe'd by tree
    suffering he's
more compassionate to bear, skunk, deer, coyote, hem-
    lock, whale
than to his own new-sprung cock. O Lizard Dharma
what doth breath, that Aums thru elm bough & rock can-
    yon loud as thru mammal skull hummed,
hymn to bone-chaliced minds now multiplied over planet
    colleges
so many, with such hollow cheek gaze-eye tenderness, Fitz-
    gerald himself'd weep to see
student faces celestial, longhaired angelic Beings planet-
    doomed to look thru too many human eyes —?
Princeton in Eternity! Long years fall, December's woods
    in snow
Old poets half century ago their bones cracked up in death
alcohol trembling in immortal eyes, Fitzgerald & Kerouac
    weeping, on earth once —
earth's voice moves thru time, old vows and prophecies
    remembered, mountain prayers repeated,
Gary's voice echoing hollow under round electric lamps.

1970

FRIDAY THE THIRTEENTH

Blasts rip Newspaper Grey Mannahatta's mid day Air Spires,
Plane roar over cloud, Sunlight on blue fleece-mist,
I travel to die, fellow passengers silk-drest & cocktailed
      burn oil NY to Chicago —
Blasting sky with big business, billion bodied Poetry Com-
      merce,
all Revolution & Consumption, Manufacture & Communi-
      cation
Bombburst, vegetable pie, rubber donut sex accessory &
      brilliant TV Jetplane CIA Joke Exorcism Fart Man-
      tra
or electronic war Laos to AID Gestapo training in Santo
      Domingo
equally massacre grass, exhaust flower power in coal facto-
      ry smokedust
—O how beautiful snowy fields earth-floored below cloud-
      holes
glimpsed from air-roads smogged thru heavens toward Illi-
      nois —
What right have I to eat petrol guns & metal from earth
      heart
What right have I to burn gas air, screech overground rub-
      ber tired round midnight stoplight corners in Peoria,
      Fort Wayne, Ames —
What prayer restores freshness to eastern meadow, soil to
      cindered acres, hemlock to rusty hillside,
transparency to Passaic streambed, Blue whale multitudes
      to coral gulfs —
What mantra bring back my mother from Madhouse, Pri-
      vate Brakefield from Leavenworth, Neal from the
      Streets of Hades,
Hampton, King, Gold, murdered suicided millions from

the War-torn fields of Sheol
where bodies twitch arm from leg torn heart beat spasmed
    brainless in dynamite Napalm rubble Song-My to
    West 11th Street Manhattan
as war bomb-blast burns along neckbone-fused nations
    Hanoi to Chicago Tu-Do to Wall Street,
Dynamite metastasis heading toward earth-brain cankering
    human world forms —
Banks burn, boys die bullet-eyed, mothers scream realiza-
    tion the vast tonnage of napalm
rolling down Grand Concourse, Fragmentation nails
    bounced off Haiphong walls
rattling machine-gunned down Halstead, the Karma of
    State Violence
washing terror-waves round earth-globe back to suburb TV
    home night kitchens
The image 3 years ago, prophetic shriek of electric screen
    dots bursting thru bathroom walls,
tile & pipes exploded in NY as on Saigon's Embassy Street
—"Northrop is favorite in hot bidding on a jet fighter for a
    fat market overseas," —*Business Week* March 7,
    1970

Earth pollution identical with Mind pollution, conscious-
    ness Pollution identical with filthy sky,
dirty-thoughted Usury simultaneous with metal dust in wa-
    ter courses
murder of great & little fish same as self besmirchment
    short hair thought control,
mace-repression of gnostic street boys identical with DDT
    extinction of Bald Eagle —
Mother's milk poisoned as fathers' thoughts, all greed-
    stained over the automobile-body designing table —

What can Poetry do, how flowers survive, how man see

right mind multitude, hear his heart's music, feel cockjoys, taste
ancient natural grain-bread and sweet vegetables, smell his own baby body's tender neck skin
when 60% State Money goes to heaven on gas clouds burning off War Machine Smokestacks?

When Violence floods the State from above, flowery land razed for robot proliferation
metal rooted & asphalted down 6 feet below topsoil,
then when bombcarrying children graduate from Grammar-school's sex-drenched gymnasia
terrified of Army Finance Meatbones, busted by cops for grassy hair,
Who can prophesy Peace, or vow Futurity for any but armed insects,
steeltip Antennaed metal soldiers porting white eggbombs where genitals were,
Blue-visor'd spray-bugs, gasmasked legions in red-brick Armory Nests —
(bearded spiders ranged under attick & roof with homebrew Arsenic mercury dung plastic readied for the Queen Bee's Immolation
in Sacramento, Trenton, Phoenix, Miami?)
The State set off a plague of bullets bombs & burning words
two decades back, & seeded Asia with Mind-thoughts excreted in Washington bathrooms —
now the Great Fear's rolled round the world & washes over Newspaper Grey air
rolling waved through cloud-smogbanks in Heaven
as the gas-burning TWA Jet house crashes thru sound barriers over Manhattan.

Chicago Chicago Chicago Trials, screams, tears, Mace, coalgas, Mafia highways—old Massacres in suburb ga-

rages!
Autos turn to water City Halls melt in Aeon-flood,
Police & revolutionaries pass as gas cloud by eagle wing.
"What's your name?" asks badge-man as machines eat all
 Name & Form,
History's faster than thought, poetry obsolete in tiny dec-
 ades tho maybe slow tunes dance eternal —
war language comes, bombblasts last a minute, coalmines
 exhaust earth-heart,
Chicago suburb blocks stretch new-bared earthskin under
 suneye,
autos speed myriad thru grey air to jet port.
Slaves of Plastic! Leather-shoe chino-pants prisoners! Hair-
 cut junkies! Dacron-sniffers!
Striped tie addicts! short hair monkeys on their backs!
 Whiskey freaks bombed out on 530 billion cigarettes
 a year —
twenty Billion dollar advertising Dealers! lipstick skin-pop-
 pers & syndicate Garbage telex-Heads!
Star-striped scoundrelesque flag-dopers! Car-smog hookers
 Fiendish on superhighways!
Growth rate trippers hallucinating Everglade real estate!
 Steak swallowers zonked on Television!
Old ladies on Stockmarket habits—old Wall Street paper
 Money-pushers!
Central Intelligence cutting Meo opium fields! China Lob-
 by copping poppies in Burma!
How long this Addict government support our oil-burner
 matter-habit
shooting gasoline electric speed before the blue light blast
 & eternal Police-roar Mankind's utter bust?
Robot airfields soulless Market electronic intelligence busi-
 ness skyscraper streets
empty-soul'd, exploding.
Sheer matter crackling, disintegrating back to void,
Sunyatta & Brahma undisturbed, Maya-cities blow up like

Chinese firecrackers,
Samsara tears itself apart—Dusk over Chicago, light-glitter
along boulevards,
insect-eyed autos moving slow under blue streetlamps,
plane motor buzz in eardrum, city cloud roof filling with
grey gas on up into clear heaven—planet horizon
auroral twilight-streaked,
blue space above human truck-moil, Empty sky
Empty mind overhanging Chicago, the universe suspended
entire overhanging Chicago.
O Jack thou'st scaped true deluge.
Smart cock, to turn to shade, I drag hairy meat loss thru
blood-red sky
down thru cloud-floor to Chicago, sunset fire obliterate in
black gas.

March 13, 1970

ANTI VIETNAM-WAR PEACE MOBILIZATION

White sunshine on sweating skulls
Washington's Monument pyramided high granite clouds
over a soul mass, children screaming in their brains on
      quiet grass
(black man strapped hanging in blue denims from an earth
      cross) —
Soul brightness under blue sky
Assembled before White House filled with mustached Ger-
      mans
& police buttons, army telephones, CIA Buzzers, FBI bugs
Secret Service walkie-talkies, Intercom squawkers to Narco
Fuzz & Florida Mafia Real Estate Speculators.
One hundred thousand bodies naked before an Iron Robot
Nixon's brain Presidential cranium case spying thru binoc-
      ulars
from the Paranoia Smog Factory's East Wing.

May 9, 1970

ECOLOGUE

In a thousand years, if there's History
America'll be remembered as a nasty little
                                    Country
full of Pricks, thorny hothouse rose
Cultivated by the Yellow Gardeners.
"Chairman Mao" for all his politics, head of a Billion
                    folk, important old & huge
            Nixon a dude, specialized on his industrial
                        Island, a clean paranoiac Mechanic —
Earth rolling round, epics on archaic tongues
                    fishermen telling island tales —
all autos rusted away,
                    trees everywhere.

        ☆   ☆   ☆   ☆   ☆

Rough Wind roar, mapletop mass
            shaking in window,
                    a panic Cry from the garden
        Bessie Cow's loose near the Corn!

The little dakini playing her bells
                & listening to late baritone Dylan
        dancing in the living room's forgot almost
                    th'electric supply's vanishing
                        from the batteries in the pasture.

Chairs shifting downstairs, kitchen voices
            Smell of apples & tomatoes bubbling on the stove.

Behind the Chicken house, dirt flies from the shovel
      hour after hour, tomorrow they'll be a big hole.

The editor sleeps in his bed, morning Chores are done,
      Clock hands move noonward, pig roots by flagstone
          pathways, papers & letters lie quiet
                    on many desks.

      Books everywhere, Kaballa, Gnostic Fragments,
Mahanirvana & Hevajra Tantras, Boehme Blake & Zohar,
Gita & Soma Veda, somebody reads—one cooks, another
digs a pighouse foundation, one chases a Cow from the
vegetable garden, one dances and sings, one writes in a
notebook, one plays with the ducks, one never speaks, one
picks the guitar, one moves huge rocks.

      The wind charger's propeller
          whirrs & trees rise windy
    one maple at woods edge's turned red.

Chickens bathe in dust at house wall,
rabbit at fence bends his nose to a handful of Cornsilk,
          fly lights on windowsill.

At the end of a long chain, Billy makes a Circle in grass
      by the fence, I approach
          he stands still with long red stick
              stretched throbbing between hind legs
      Spurts water a minute, turns his head down
            to look & lick his thin pee squirt —
        That's why he smells goat like.

Horse by barbed wire licking salt,
                    lifts his long head & neighs
          as I go down by willow thicket
                    to find the 3-day-old heifer.
At bed in long grass, wet brown fur —
her mother stands, nose covered with a hundred flies.

The well's filled up —
                    the Cast-iron ram
                that pushes water uphill
                        by hydraulic pressure
                                flowed from gravity
          Can be set to motion soon,
                    & water flow in kitchen sink tap.

Some nights in sleeping bag
          Cricket zinging networks dewy meadows,
          white stars sparkle across black sky,
falling asleep I listen & watch
          till eyes close, and wake silent —
                at 4 AM the whole sky's moved,
a Crescent moon lamps up the woods.

& last week one Chill night
                        summer disappeared —
          little apples in old trees red,
                tomatoes red & green on vines,
          green squash huge under leafspread,
                    corn thick in light green husks,
          sleepingbag wet with dawn dews
                    & that one tree red at woods' edge!

Louder wind! ther'll be electric to play the Beatles!

At summer's end the white pig got so fat
                    it weighed more than Georgia
                            Ray Bremser's 3-year-old baby.
        Scratch her named Dont Bite Me under hind leg,
                she flops over on her side sweetly grunting,
                nosing in grass tuft roots, soft belly warm.

Eldridge Cleaver exiled w/ bodyguards in Algiers
Leary sleeping in an iron cell,
                    John Sinclair a year jailed in Marquette
Each day's paper more violent —
                War outright shameless bombs
                            Indochina to Minneapolis —
        a knot in my belly to read between lines,
                    lies, beatings in jail —
                    Short breath on the couch —
    desolation at dawn in bed —
                    Wash dishes in the sink, drink tea,
                                boil an egg —
            brood over Cities' suffering millions two
                                hundred miles away
                down the oilslicked, germ-Chemicaled
                            Hudson river.

Ed Hermit comes down hill
        breaks off a maple branch
        & offers fresh green leaves to the pink eyed rabbit.

Under birch, yellow mushrooms
            ·   sprout between grassblades & ragweed —
        Eat 'em & you die or get high & see God —
                Waiting for the exquisite mycologist's visit.

Winter's coming, build a rough wood crib
      & fill it with horse dung, hot horse dung,
          all round the house sides.

Bucolics & Eclogues!
      Hesiod the beginning of the World,
          Virgil the end of his World —
& Catullus sucked cock in the country
          far from the Emperor's police.

Empire got too big, cities too crazy, garbage-filled Rome
          full of drunken soldiers, fat politicians,
              circus businessmen —
      Safer, healthier life on a farm, make yr own wine
          in Italy, smoke yr own grass in America.

Pond's down two feet from drainpipe's rusty top —
Timothy turned brown, covered with new spread manure
          sweet smelt in strong breeze,
              it'll be covered in snow couple months.
      & Leary covered in snow in San Luis Obispo jail?
          His mind snowflakes falling over the States.

Did Don Winslow the mason come look at the basement
      So we can insulate a snug root cellar
          for potatoes, beets, carrots,
             radishes, parsnips, glass jars of corn & beans
Did the mortician come & look us over for next Winter?

Black flies walking up and down the metal screen,
          fly's leg tickling my forehead —
      "I'll play a fly's bone flute
      & beat an ant's egg drum"

                              sang the Quechua Injun
                              high on Huilca snuff, Peruvian
                                  Mediaeval DMT.

Phil Whalen in Japan
                    stirring rice, eyes in the garden,
                              fine pen nib lain by notebook.

Jack in Lowell farming worms, master of his
                              miniscule deep acre.

Neal's ashes sitting under a table piled with
                    books, in an oak drawer,
                              sunlight thru suburb windows.

O wind! spin the generator wheel, make Power Juice
To run the New Exquisite Noise Recorder, & I'll sing
                    praise of your tree music.

Squash leaves wave & ragweeds lean, black tarpaulin
              plastic flutters over the bass-wood lumber pile
          Hamilton Fish's Congressional letter
                    reports "Stiffer laws against peddling smut"
          flapping in dusty spiderwebs by the windowscreen.

What's the Ammeter read by the Windmill? Will
              we record *Highest Perfect Wisdom* all day tomorrow,
              or Blake's *Schoolboy* uninterrupted next week?

Fine rain-slant showering the grey porch
                    Returnable Ginger Ale Bottles
                              on the wood rail, white paint flaked
                                  off into orange flowered
                                      blossoms

Out in the garden, rain
      all over the grass, leaves, roofs,
           rain on the laundry.

      ★   ★   ★

Night winds hiss thru maple black masses
Gas light shine from ·
      farmhouse window upstairs
    empty kitchen wind
Cassiopeia zigzag
      Milky Way thru cloud

September 4

The baby pig screamed and screamed
      four feet rigid on grass
      screamed and screamed
          Oh No! Oh No!
      jaw dripping blood
          broken by the horse's hoof.
  Slept in straw all afternoon, eyes closed,
      snout at rest between paws —
    ate hog mash liquid—two weeks
          and his skull be healed
      said the Vet in overalls.

That bedraggled duck's sat under the door
      June to Labor Day, three hatched
          yellow chicks' dry fur bones found
           by the garage side —

154

two no-good eggs left, nights chillier —
Next week, move her nest
to the noisy chickenhouse.

We buried lady dog by the apple tree —
spotted puppy daughter Radha
sniffed her bloated corpse, flies
whisping round eyeball & dry nostril,
sweet rot-smell, stiff legs, anus puffed out,
Sad Eyes chased the milk truck & got killed.

How many black corpses they found in the river
looking for Goodman, Chaney, Schwerner?

Man and wife, they weep in the attic
after bitter voices,
low voices threatening.

Broken Legs in Vietnam!
Eyes staring at heaven,
Eyes weeping at earth.
Millions of bodies in pain!
Who can live with this Consciousness
and not wake frightened at sunrise?

The Farm's a lie!
Madmen growing giant organic zucchini
mulching asparagus, boiling tomatoes for Winter,
drying beans, pickling cucumbers
sweet & garlicked, salting cabbage for sauerkraut,
canning fresh corn & tossing Bessie husks —
Marie Antoinette had milkmaid costumes ready,
Robespierre's eyeball hung on his cheek
in the tumbril to guillotine —

Black Panther's teeth knocked out in Paterson,
            red blood clotted on black hairy skin —
                        Millions of bodies in pain!

One by one picked orange striped soft potato bugs off
                              withered brown leaves
            dropped them curl'd up in kerosene,
      or smeared them on ground with small stones —

Moon rocket earth photo, peacock colored,
                              tacked to the wood wall,
            globe in black sky
                        living eyeball bathed in cloud swirls —
                              Is Earth herself frightened?
                                    Does she know?
Oh No! Oh No! the Continuous scream
                  of the pig
                        Dont Bite Me in the backyard,
                        bloody jawbone askew.

Uphill on pine forest floor
            Indian peace pipes curl'd up thru dry needles,
            half translucent fungus, half metal blossom

Frog sat half out on mud shallows'
                  minnow-rippling surface,
                        & stared at our Universe —
So many fish frog, insect ephemera, swamp fern
      —So many Ezekiel-wheeled Dragonflies
                  hovering over old Hemlock root moss —
            They wont even know when humans go

Waking 2 AM clock tick
            What was I dreaming

my body alert
Police light down this dirt road?
            Justice Dogs sniffing field for Grass Seeds?
    Would they find a little brown mushroom button
                            tossed out my window?
                FBI read this haiku?

Four in the morning
                rib thrill eyes open —
                        Deep hum thru the house —
            Windmill Whir? Hilltop Radar Blockhouse?
                    Valley Traffic 5 miles downtown?
    When'll Policecar Machinery assemble
                            outside State pine woods?
            Head out window—bright Orion star line,
                Pleiades and Dipper shining silent —

Bathrobe flashlight, uproad Milky Way
            Moved round the house this month
        —remember Taurus' Horn up there last fall?
White rabbit on goat meadow, got over the chickenwire?
        Hop away from flash light? Wait till Godly
                            Dog wakes up!
Come back! He'll bite you! Here's a green beet leaf!
                    Pwzxst! Pwzxst! Pwzxst!

Attic window lit between trees,
            Clouds drift past the sickle moon —
Tiny lights in the dark sky
                        Stars & Crickets everywhere
                        Electric whistle-blinks
                            tweedle-twinks
                                Squeak-peeks

Locust planet
zephyr sizzle
Squinks —
Grasshoppers in cold dewy fall grass
Singing lovesongs as they die.

★   ★   ★

Morning, the white rabbit stiff, eyes closed,
lain belly up in grass, tooth nosed,
beside the manure pile—dig a hole
—Shoulda introduced him to dogs in daylight —

Cripple Jack drove up
to judge the ducks —
All eggs sterile,
smashed on rock, wet guts
& rotted-throat smell —
Bedraggled duck mother,
dragged off straw nest
& pecking skin at my wrist,
All afternoon walked up and down quacking
thru chickenwire fence

Pig on her side woke up,
slurped beet juice, rooted at porch wood
ignorant of broken head bones —

Morning dew, papery leafs & sharp blossoms
of sunflower ripped off battered stalks,
Who'd do that!? Too late
to fix the barbedwire fence,
intelligent Bessie Cow strays in the moonlight.

Leary's climbed the chainlink fence & two strands of
barbedwire too
This weekend, "Armed & Dangerous,"
Signed with Weathermen!
Has Revolution begun? World War III?
May no Evil Eye peek thru window, keyhole or
gunsight at his white haired face!

Now's halfmoon over America,
leaves tinged red fall blush scattered overhill,
down pasture singular trees orange foreheads think
Autumn time in pines —
The maple at woods' edge fire-red's brighter
Australian Aborigines' Eternal Dream Time's come true —
Usta be bears on East Hill; fox under old Hemlock,
Usta be otter—even woolly mammoths in Eternal
dream time —
Leary's out in the woods of the world—cockroaches immune
to radiation?
Richard Nixon has means to end human Worlds,
Man has machines for Suicide,
Pray for Timothy Leary in the planet's Woods!
Om Mani Padme Hūṃ
& Hare Krishna!
"As we forgive those who trespass against us,
Thy Will be done
on Earth as in Heaven"
Oh Bessie you ate my unborn sunflowers!
"God never repeats himself" Harry Smith telephoned
tonite.

We may not come back, Richard Nixon.
We may not come back, dear hidden Tim.

Will Peter fix the sink's hand pump? the basement freeze?
  Backyard grasses stink, if kitchen drains
      to septic tank, will Bacteria die
        of soap, Ammonia & Kerosene?

Get rid of that old tractor or fix it!
      Cardboard boxes rotten in garageside rain!
Old broken City desks under the appletree! Cleanum
      up for firewood!
Where can we keep all summer's bottles?
     Gas pumps, broken mandolins, old tires —
       Ugly backyard—Shelf the garage!
  Where stack lumber handy to eye?
Electric generator money? Where keep mops in Wintertime?

Leary fugitive, Sinclair sent up for a decade —
    though 83% of World's illegal opium's fixed
  in Central Intelligence Agency's Indochinese Brain!
    Fed State Local Narcs peddle junk —
      Nixon got a hard hat from Mafia,
Pentagon Public Relations boodle's 190 million A.D. 1969.
     J. E. Hoover's a sexual blackmailer,
      Times pities "idealistic students"
       Police killed 4 Blacks in New Orleans
Fascism in America: —
  i.e. Police control Cities, not Mayors or philosophers —
   Police, & Police alone, cause most crime.
 Preventative Detention now law in D.C.
 Mexico & Senegal close borders to Adam Longhair

So many apples in abandoned orchards,
        and such fresh sweet Cider, supper tonite —
            onions & cabbage fried on iron —
      groundwells overflow, hydraulic ram
                works steady again,
Eclogues! the town laundry's detergent phosphate
      glut's foul'd clear Snyders Creek —
      I have a beautiful boy in the house,
      learn keyboard notation, chords, & improvise
         freely on Blake's mantras at midnite.
Hesiod annaled Beginnings
      I annal ends for No man.

Hail to the Gods, who are given Consciousness.
Hail to Men Conscious of the Gods!

Electric tempest!
        Entire hillsides turned wet gold,
          Leaf death's begun, universal September
               Emerges in old maples
Goat bells near the house, not much in the
          garden they can eat now anyway,
     & cow got beet tops and mangles already —
            What do dogs hear?
Birds squeak & chatter as Rooster call
      echoes round house wall

Civilization's breaking down! Freezertray's
      lukewarm, who knows why?
The year-old Toilet's leaking at the heel—Wind
     Charger's so feeble batteries are almost down —
Hundreds of black spotted tomatoes
      waiting near the kitchen wood stove
"Useless! useless! the heavy rain driving into the sea!"

Kerouac, Cassady, Olson ash & earth, Leary the Irish
           coach on the lam,
Black Magicians screaming in anger Newark to Algiers,
How many bottles & cans piled up in our garbagepail?

Fall 1970

GURU OM

October 4, 1970

Car wheels roar over freeway concrete
Night falls on Dallas, two buildings shine under sickle
　　　moon
Many boys and girls in jail for their bodies poems and
　　　bitter thoughts
My belly's hollow breath sighs up thru my heart
Guru Om Guru Om enlarges in the vast space of the breast
The Guru has a man's brown belly and cock long hair
　　　white beard short hair orange hat no person
The bliss alone no business for my body but to make Guru
　　　Om dwell near my heart
shall I telephone New York and tell my fellows where I am
　　　silent
shall I ring my own head & order my own voice to be
　　　silent but
How giant, silent and feather-soft is the cave of my body
　　　eyes closed　　　　　　　　　　·
To enter the body is difficult, the belly's full of bad smell-
　　　ing wind
the body's digesting last weekend's meat thinking of Ciga-
　　　rettes, bright eyes of boys
What Acid eight hours equals eight hours' Om continuous
　　　attention —
the Guru is equal to the Om of the Seeker
Guru Guru Guru Guru Guru Guru Guru Citaram Omkar
　　　Das Thakur thin voic'd recommended "Give up
　　　desire for children"
Dehorahava Baba sat on the Ganges and described eat &
　　　drinking pranayam

Nityananda floated thru his giant photo body
Babaji's hand the hand of a dead man in my dead man's
        fingers
Out the plane window brown gas rises to heaven's blue sea
—how end the poetry movie in the mind?
how tell Kabir Blake & Ginsberg shut their ears?
Folded in silence invisible Guru waits to fill his body with
        Emptiness
I am leaving the world, I will close my eyes & rest my
        tongue and hand.

October 5, 1970

To look in the City without hatred
the orange moon edge sunk into blue Cloud
a second night autos roar to and fro Downtown towers'
        horizon
airplane moving between moon and white-lit bank towers
lightning haze above twinkling-bulbed man city flats
It is mind-City risen particularly solid.
What elder age grew such cities visioned from these far
        towers' windows
Seraph armchaired in Babylonic Déjà Vu from Hilton Inn?

October 6, 1970

Dallas buildings' heaped rock tangled steel electric lit un-
        der quarter moon
Cars crash at dusk at Mockingbird Lane, Drugstore Super-
        market signs revolve with dumb beckoning persist-
        ence over North Central Freeway

Leary leaped over the wall with a sword, Errol Flynn's in
the grave, flags & bombs fly over Dallas' stock ex-
change
oil flows thru the Hilton Faucets, gasoline fumes smother
Neem trees in Ganeshpuri —
Maya revolves on rubber wheels, Samsara's glass buildings
light up with neon; Illusion's doors open on alumi-
num hinges —
my mother should've done asanas & Kundalini not
straightjackets & Electroshock in the birthdays of
Roosevelt's FBI —
Where in the body's the white thumbsize subtle corpus, in
the neck they say
where's the half-thumbjoint black causal body, down in
the heart hidden?
where's the lentil-sized Cosmic Corpse, a tiny blue speck in
the navel?
All beings at war in the Gross body, armor Cars & Na-
palm, rifles & grass huts burning, Mace on Wall
Street, tear gas flooding the fallen stockmarket.
Look in halls of the head, *nervous leg halls,* universe inside
Chest dark baby kingdom in the skull.

"HAVE YOU SEEN THIS MOVIE?"

Old maple hairytrunks root asphalt grass marge, November
      branches rare leaved,
Giant woodlegged wiretowers' threads stretch above pond
      woods highway, white sun fallen hills West.
Car rolling underpass, radio hornvoice "the sight of Bobby
      Seale bound & gagged at Trial" denied lawyer pre-
      sum'd innocent?
MDA Love Drug Cure Junk Habit? Rochester Exit one
      mile flashing out Volkswagen window —
Blue sky fring'd with clouds' whale-ghost-blue schools
      north drift —
High, high Manson sighed on Trial, how many folk in jail
      for grass Ask Congressman?
Highway Crash! Politics! Police! Dope! armed robbery
      Customary E. 10th street, no insurance possible.
—Brown deer tied neat footed dead eye horned across blue
      Car trunk, old folks Front seat, they're gonna eat it!
Help! Hurrah! What's Going on here? Samsara? Illusion?
      Reality?
What're all these trailers row'd up hillside, more people?
      How can Lyca sleep?
Cows on Canandaigua fields lactate into rubber stainless
      steel plastic milkhouse machinery vats ashine —
Revolutionary Suicide! Driving on Persian gasoline?
Kill Whale & ocean? Oh one American myself shits 1000
      times more Chemical waste into freshwater & seas
      than any single Chinaman!
America Suicide Cure World Cancer! Myself included de-
      pendent on Chemicals, wheels, dollars.
metal Coke Cans Liquid propane batteries marijuana let-
      tuce avocados cigarettes plastic pens & milkbot-
      tles—electric

in N.Y.C. heavy habit, cut airconditioners isolation from
    street nightmare smog heat study decentralized
    Power sources 10 years
not atomic thermopollutive monolith. Om. How many
    species poisoned biocided from Earth realms?
O bald Eagle & Blue Whale with giant piteous Cat
    Squeak—Oh Wailing whale ululating underocean's
    sonic roar of Despair!
Sing thy Kingdom to Language deaf America! Scream thy
    black Cry thru Radio electric Aether —
Scream in Death America! Or did Captain Ahab not
    scream Curses as he hurled harpoon
into the body of the mother, great White Whale Nature
    Herself,
thrashing in intelligent agony innocent vast in the oil-can
    sick waters?
All Northvietnam bomb-Cratered ruined topsoil Laos in
    secrecy more bombs than many W W II's!
Mekong swamp lethacided by Monsanto Pentagon
    Academy Death-brains!
What wisdom teaching this? What Mafia runs N.J.? What
    Mafia knew J. Edgar FBI?
What's Schenley's Whiskey trader Fleischman's Hoover In-
    stitute?
What opium's passed thru CIA Agents' airplane's luggage in
    Saigon, Bangkok, Athens, Washington?
What narcotic agent's not dependent on Shit for a living?
What Bank's money created ex nihil serves orphan, widow,
    monk, philosopher?
or what Bank's money serves real Estate Asphalt over
    widow's garden? Serves old Nick in the Pentagon?
Old Indian prophecies believe Ghost Dance peace will
    Come restore prairie Buffalo or great White Father
    Honkie
be trampled to death in his dreams by returning herds'

thundering reincarnation!

Oh awful Man! What have we made the world! Oh man capitalist exploiter of Mother Planet!

Oh vain insect sized men with metal slaves by Great Lake Erie, tenderest Passaic & Hudson poisoned by dollars!

BID TAMPERING PROBED IN LACKAWANNA *Buffalo News* headline folded on rubber floor, car vibrating smooth to sun ruddy woods' dusk quiet —

Radio hissing cough words dashboard noisemusic—Any minute Apocalypse Rock!

Brown Pelican eggs softened by DDT. Seal's livers poisoned to Northman. Oceans Dead 2000 AD.

Television Citizen 6% Earths human Americans ingest half the planet's raw matter as alchemized by Syracuse Gen. Electric Power brown robot palace near 8 Lane Thruway's Exit before Ramada Inn.

HXL Trucks sleeping on brokenearthed embankment past Iron-strutted passages,

fields aglitter with damp metallic garbage under th'electricwire trestles —

And woods survived into another Thanksgiving's brown sacred silence —

Lights on cars front Western Lane grey twilight falls on rolling robotland.

November 1970

MILAREPA TASTE

Who am I? Saliva,
   vegetable soup,
       empty mouth?

Hot roach, breathe smoke
   suck in, hold, exhale —
      light as ashes.

OVER LARAMIE

Western Air boat bouncing
    under rainclouds stippled
        down grey Rockies
            Springtime dusk,
Look out on Denver, Allen,
      mourn Neal no more,
    Old ghost bone loves departed
    New lives whelm the plains, rains
        wash Rocky mountainsides
World turns under sun eye
    Man flies a moment Cheyenne's
      dry upland highways
A tiny fossil brachiapod in pocket
    Precambrian limestone clam
          fingernail small
four hundred fifty million years old

Brain gone, flesh passed thru myriad
    phantom reincarnations,
the tiny-ridged shell's
      delicate as hardened thought.
—over Laramie, Front Range
    pine gully snow pockets,
Monolith Cement plume smoke
    casting dust gas over
      the red plateau
    into the New World.

April 12, 1971

V

Bixby Canyon to Jessore Road

1971

BIXBY CANYON OCEAN PATH WORD BREEZE

Tiny orange-wing-tipped butterfly
fluttering sunlit
from violet
blossom to violet
blossom

Ocean is private
you have to visit
her to see her
Garden undercliff
      Dewey Pinks,
        bitter Mint,
     Sea Sage,
       Orange flaming
          Paintbrush
   greenspiked fleurs,
  Thick dainty stalked
       Cow Parsley,
Starleaf'd violet bushes,
yelloweyed blue
      Daisy clump —
red brambled mature sour
          blackberry briars,
yellow budded
       Lupine
    nodding stalkheads
    in Sunwarm'd
       breezes
by the brooks tricklet
    wash in the ravine
        Bridged with cloud

Ruddy withwine morning
  glory's tiny tender
      cowbells,
  guarded by poison oak sprigs
      oily hands
Green horned little
   British chickweed,
waxlight-leafed black
     seed stalk's
  lilac sweet budcluster
Ah fluted morning
  glory bud
    oped
& tickled to yellow
  tubed stamen root
  by a six legged
   armed mite
  deeping his head
  into sweet pollened
     crotches,
Crawls up yr veined
  blossom wall
  to petal lip in
   sunshine clear
  and dives again
  to your tongue-stamen's
   foot-pipe, your
  bloom unfolded
  to light —

   Above ye the
   Spider's left
   his one strand
    catgut silk

                    shining
                        bridge
            between
                cookoospitted
                    mint leafheads
            & newgreen leafsprig'd
                    seedy lilac
Granite Sagely
    Browed above the Path's
        black pepper peapod marge —
Grey rock dropping
        seed,
withered bush-fingers
        tangled up
        stoneface
        —cracked with
        green stalk
                sprout —
Brooktrickle deep
    below Airplane
            Bridge
                Concrete
        arches balconey'd
    Pendant over
Oceancrash
        waves
falling empty eyed
    breathing water
            wash afar

Morning Night shade
    in alder shadow'd
Pathside—Nettle plant
    Leaf-shoulder
    vegetable wing'd

baby faces,
green earmouths
sprouting
Celery handspread
Heal-All mudras
open asking why me.

Sunlight trembling
branch-leafy willow,
yellow haired wingy bee's
black horn
bowed into threadpackt mauve
round thistle mouth,
dewey web throat
green needle collar'd,
Symmetric little
Cathead erect
electric thorn'd
under giant hogweed
stalked parasol blossoms —

Ash branch's tender
pinecone cluster
proffered by leathery
sawtooth rib leafs

red browed beedle
perched on Egyptian
bridge of Spider fern's
soft-jointed spike-sticks
Brown water
streaming
underbrush
sparrowsong

       winged brown
       whistling above
cold water pebble
      silver pour . . .
Shrowded
   under the
Ash spread, on
   damp leafwither,
shield tubes
    & condensers
       of small Sony
      TV machine enwired
      rusty w/resistences

   giant grass
     leafspears
morning glory hillside
    perched over clearing
All branches lifting
      up
   papery seedhusks,

parasolspiked Fern
    Tramping together
      upright pushing
       a thistle aside,
    groundwheat leaned
   by beach path —

Oh ocean white-
    waved pouring
  foamy noises over
    rocky sandshore
Chevrolet writ

on radiatormouth
Set above
    Private Land
Do Not Enter
  incised wood
    Sign-beams

net wt. 68 LB   class 6   hear
net wt. 68LB   class 6
601170   head 20

          T

    Ice
  Packed
ready to cook

FRYING CHICKENS

with giblets

INSPECTED FOR WHOLESOMENESS

BY U.S. DEPARTMENT OF AGRICULTURE

P - 550

processed by PETERSON INDUSTRIES, INC.
             DECATUR, ARK.
             U.S.A. 72722.

Frying chickens from
  Arkansas!

Musselshells'
    Briared graveyard
        footplot —
Dewey round bushes
    guarding ocean
        path with
    myriad greenstar'd
        leafarms
    cradling white-walled
        dewdrops

Telephone
    pole trunk
stuck
    out of old
    landslide head
    Covered with iceplant
    green lobsterclaw
        trefoil solid
            edged,
    pinked with
    hundredfingerpetaled
        Sea vine blossoms
Dry brown kelp
    ribs washed
    in a heap at
    streamside in
        wet brown sand
        to listen to
        . oceanroar
        and wait the
        slow moon
            tide.

Stream water
   rushing flat through
beachmound
   Sand precipices,
tiny wet arizonas
flood lips
       —cliffs
cradling the last
   greysmooth boulders
   shat by the rains
pissed out
   by spring storm
     from
the forests
       bladder
       hills
   Small granite
   blackpocked
    hearthstones
   washed to last rest
   Ocean wavelet's
      salt tongue
      touching
      forward thru
       sand throated
      streambed
       to lave foam &
      pull back bubbles
      from the iron
   Car's rusty
     under carriage
       kelp pipes
         & brown chassis,

               one rubber wheel
                  black poked from
                     Sand mattresses
                        rock wash
O Kerouac
      thy broken
      car Behold
    Digested in
    Saltwater
        sandbottom
   giant soulless
      Chicken
        sea gizzard filled
           with unthinking
      marble rocks —
   Poured down
     road in
       avalanche!
  to the granite
    snout of the
         seacliff

O see the great
        Snake kelp's
   beet green head still lettuce-
              haired
     stretch forth
        a fingerthick tailroot
above seaweed broider
        wavelets
    rushing foam
          tongued —
Was that kelp
    Intelligent

Einstein hairleafed
        faceless bulbhead

Oh father
        Welcome!
    The seal's
        head lifted
    above the wave,
    eyes watching
        from black
                face
    in waterfroth
            floating!
    Come back again!

Huge white
waves rolling
in grey mist
birds flocking
    rocks foamed
    floating above
    the
        horizon's
            watery
                wrinkled
                    skin
    grandmother
        oceanskirt
                rumbling
                    pebbles
        silver hair ear to ear.

May 28, 1971

HŪM BOM!

Whom bomb?
We bomb them!
Whom bomb?
We bomb them!
Whom bomb?
We bomb them!
Whom bomb?
We bomb them!

Whom bomb?
You bomb you!
Whom bomb?
You bomb you!
Whom bomb?
You bomb you!
Whom Bomb?
You bomb you!

What do we do?
Who do we bomb?
What do we do?
Who do we bomb?
What do we do?
Who do we bomb?
What do we do!
Who do we bomb?

What do we do?
You bomb! You bomb them!
What do we do?
You bomb! You bomb them!
What do we do?

We bomb! We bomb them!
What do we do?
We bomb! We bomb them!

Whom bomb?
We bomb you!
Whom bomb?
We bomb you!
Whom bomb?
You bomb you!
Whom bomb?
You bomb you!

May 71

SEPTEMBER ON JESSORE ROAD

Millions of babies watching the skies
Bellies swollen, with big round eyes
On Jessore Road—long bamboo huts
Noplace to shit but sand channel ruts

Millions of fathers in rain
Millions of mothers in pain
Millions of brothers in woe
Millions of sisters nowhere to go

One Million aunts are dying for bread
One Million uncles lamenting the dead
Grandfather millions homeless and sad
Grandmother millions silently mad

Millions of daughters walk in the mud
Millions of children wash in the flood
A Million girls vomit & groan
Millions of families hopeless alone

Millions of souls Nineteenseventyone
homeless on Jessore road under grey sun
A million are dead, the millions who can
Walk toward Calcutta from East Pakistan

Taxi September along Jessore Road
Oxcart skeletons drag charcoal load
past watery fields thru rain flood ruts
Dung cakes on treetrunks, plastic-roof huts

Wet processions   Families walk
Stunted boys   big heads dont talk
Look bony skulls   & silent round eyes
Starving black angels in human disguise

Mother squats weeping & points to her sons
Standing thin legged   like elderly nuns
small bodied   hands to their mouths in prayer
Five months small food   since they settled there

on one floor mat   with a small empty pot
Father lifts up his hands at their lot
Tears come to their mother's eye
Pain makes mother Maya cry

Two children together   in palmroof shade
Stare at me   no word is said
Rice ration, lentils   one time a week
Milk powder for warweary infants meek

No vegetable money or work for the man
Rice lasts four days   eat while they can
Then children starve   three days in a row
and vomit their next food   unless they eat slow.

On Jessore road   Mother wept at my knees
Bengali tongue   cried mister Please
Identity card   torn up on the floor
Husband still waits   at the camp office door

Baby at play I was washing the flood
Now they won't give us any more food
The pieces are here in my celluloid purse
Innocent baby play   our death curse

Two policemen surrounded   by thousands of boys
Crowded waiting   their daily bread joys
Carry big whistles   & long bamboo sticks
to whack them in line   They play hungry tricks

Breaking the line   and jumping in front
Into the circle   sneaks one skinny runt
Two brothers dance forward   on the mud stage
The guards blow their whistles   & chase them in rage

Why are these infants   massed in this place
Laughing in play   & pushing for space
Why do they wait here so cheerful   & dread
Why this is the House where they give children bread

The man in the bread door   Cries & comes out
Thousands of boys & girls   Take up his shout
Is it joy? is it prayer?   "No more bread today"
Thousands of Children at once scream   "Hooray!"

Run home to tents   where elders await
Messenger children   with bread from the state
No bread more today! & no place to squat
Painful baby, sick shit he has got.

Malnutrition skulls thousands for months
Dysentery drains   bowels all at once
Nurse shows disease card   Enterostrep
Suspension is wanting   or else chlorostrep

Refugee camps   in hospital shacks
Newborn lay naked   on mother's thin laps
Monkeysized week-old   Rheumatic babe eye
Gastroenteritis Blood Poison   thousands must die

September Jessore   Road rickshaw
50,000 souls   in one camp I saw
Rows of bamboo   huts in the flood
Open drains, & wet families waiting for food

Border trucks flooded, food cant get past,
American Angel machine   please come fast!
Where is Ambassador Bunker today?
Are his Helios machinegunning children at play?

Where are the helicopters of U.S. AID?
Smuggling dope in Bangkok's green shade.
Where is America's Air Force of Light?
Bombing North Laos all day and all night?

Where are the President's Armies of Gold?
Billionaire Navies   merciful Bold?
Bringing us medicine   food and relief?
Napalming North Viet Nam   and causing more grief?

Where are our tears? Who weeps for this pain?
Where can these families go in the rain?
Jessore Road's children close their big eyes
Where will we sleep when Our Father dies?

Whom shall we pray to for rice and for care?
Who can bring bread to this shit flood foul'd lair?
Millions of children alone in the rain!
Millions of children weeping in pain!

Ring O ye tongues of the world for their woe
Ring out ye voices for Love we dont know
Ring out ye bells of electrical pain
Ring in the conscious American brain

How many children are we who are lost
Whose are these daughters we see turn to ghost?
What are our souls that we have lost care?
Ring out ye musics and weep if you dare —

Cries in the mud by the thatch'd house sand drain
Sleeps in huge pipes in the wet shit-field rain
waits by the pump well, Woe to the world!
whose children still starve   in their mother's arms curled.

Is this what I did to myself in the past?
What shall I do Sunil Poet I asked?
Move on and leave them without any coins?
What should I care for the love of my loins?

What should we care for our cities and cars?
What shall we buy with our Food Stamps on Mars?
How many millions sit down in New York
& sup this night's table on bone & roast pork?

How many million beer cans are tossed
in Oceans of Mother? How much does She cost?
Cigar gasolines and   asphalt car dreams
Stinking the world and dimming star beams —

Finish the war in your breast   with a sigh
Come taste the tears   in your own Human eye
Pity us millions of phantoms you see
Starved in Samsara   on planet TV

How many millions of children die more
before our Good Mothers perceive the Great Lord?
How many good fathers pay tax to rebuild
Armed forces that boast   the children they've killed?

How many souls walk through Maya in pain
How many babes   in illusory rain?
How many families   hollow eyed lost?
How many grandmothers   turning to ghost?

How many loves who never get bread?
How many Aunts with holes in their head?
How many sisters skulls on the ground?
How many grandfathers   make no more sound?

How many fathers in woe
How many sons   nowhere to go?
How many daughters   nothing to eat?
How many uncles   with swollen sick feet?

Millions of babies in pain
Millions of mothers in rain
Millions of brothers in woe
Millions of children   nowhere to go

November 14-16 1971

AFTER WORDS

Beginning with "long poem of these States," *The Fall of America* continues *Planet News* chronicle taperecorded scribed by hand or sung condensed, the flux of car bus airplane dream consciousness Person during Automated Electronic War years, newspaper headline radio brain auto poesy & silent desk musings, headlights flashing on road through these States of consciousness. Texts here dedicated to Whitman Good Grey Poet complement otherwhere published *Wichita Vortex Sutra* and *Iron Horse*. The book enters Northwest border thence down California Coast Xmas 1965 and wanders East to include history epic in Kansas & Bayonne, mantra chanting in Cleveland smoke flats, Great Lake hotel room midnight soliloquies, defeatest prophetics Nebraskan, sociable kissass in Houston, sexist gay rhapsodies, elegy for love friend poet heroes threaded through American silver years, pacifist-vowelled changes of self in robot city, wavecrash babbling & prayers airbourne, reportage Presidentiad Chicago police-state teargas eye, car crash body consciousness, ecologue inventory over Atlantic seabord's iron Megalopolis & west desert's smogtinged Vast. Back home, Mannahatta's garbaged loves survive, farm country without electricity falltime harvest's the illegal Indochina bomb paranoia guilt. Guru Om meditation breaks through onto empty petrochemical wonderland, & so adieu to empty-lov'd America. Book returns to Pacific flowered seashore with antibomb call, then across ocean great suffering starvation's visible, bony human *September on Jessore Road* ends as mantric lamentation rhymed for vocal chant to western chords F minor B flat E flat B flat.

Allen Ginsberg

October 7, 1972